The Hebrew Prophets

Other books in the
SkyLight Illuminations Series

The Hebrew Prophets

Selections Annotated & Explained

Translation & Annotation
by Rabbi Rami Shapiro

Foreword by Rabbi Zalman Schachter-Shalomi

Walking Together, Finding the Way
SKYLIGHT PATHS Publishing
Woodstock, Vermont

The Hebrew Prophets:
Selections Annotated & Explained

2004 First Printing

Translation, annotation, and introductory material © 2004 by Rami Shapiro

Library of Congress Cataloging-in-Publication Data

Bible. O.T. Prophets. English. Shapiro. Selections. 2004.
The Hebrew prophets : selections annotated & explained /
translation & annotation by Rami Shapiro ; foreword by Zalman M. Schachter-
Shalomi
p. cm. — (SkyLight illuminations series)
Includes bibliographical references.
ISBN 1-59473-037-7 (pbk.)
1. Bible. O.T. Prophets—Criticism, interpretation, etc. I.
Shapiro, Rami M. II. Title. III. SkyLight illuminations.
BS1503.S53 2004
224'.05209—dc22   2004013778

10 9 8 7 6 5 4 3 2 1
Manufactured in the United States of America

SkyLight Paths, "Walking Together, Finding the Way," and colophon are trademarks
of LongHill Partners, Inc., registered in the U.S. Patent and Trademark Office.

Walking Together, Finding the Way
Published by SkyLight Paths Publishing
A Division of LongHill Partners, Inc.
Sunset Farm Offices, Route 4, P.O. Box 237
Woodstock, VT 05091
Tel: (802) 457-4000   Fax: (802) 457-4004
www.skylightpaths.com

Contents ☐

Foreword: The Prophet of Bellevue □

Zalman Schachter-Shalomi

Around 1962 I was reading the New York edition of the *Jewish Post* and came across a headline that read, "These Words Got a Person Committed to Bellevue Hospital." Inside was reprinted a little leaflet that someone had written and distributed in mimeographed copies. It was an indictment of modern Jews and Judaism, which read, "You have fancy synagogues, but there is no God there…. You are dressing your daughters in such a way that they will have a real difficulty in being chaste…. You claim to honor me, but you honor not the needs of the poor." Here was Isaiah's "Is this the fast that I have chosen" in modern language from a man called "Eliezer, the Servant of the Lord," a modern Jewish prophet.

I was so interested in this man that I called Charlie Roth, who had written the article for the *Jewish Post*, and asked him some questions about this Eliezer. Charlie's article told of how he had "bailed Eliezer out" of Bellevue mental hospital, and I wanted to know more. I asked him, "What's the story with this guy?"

"He has been told by God that he must do this work and speak these words," Charlie responded.

What had happened was this: One day Eliezer was standing in front of Congregation Emanu-El in New York distributing his leaflets. With each one he gave away he would say, "Please don't litter by throwing this in the street. If you don't want it, just hand it back to me." At first the people at Congregation Emanu-El figured he was a Christian and wondered if they should even bother with him. But as they didn't see anything about

Jesus in the material, they suspected he might be Jewish and took one of the fliers to the rabbi. The rabbi read it and was incensed by it. The people of Congregation Emanu-El called the police, and the police called an ambulance from Bellevue.

The ambulance arrived and Eliezer refused to get in, saying, "This is not what God has asked me to do." They picked him up bodily and put him in the ambulance. That was the first day of Rosh HaShannah.

For two days he neither spoke nor took food from his "jailors." On the second evening Eliezer finally broke his silence by saying, "I'm entitled to a phone call." They asked him, "What's the number? We'll dial it for you." He closed his eyes for a moment and then gave them the contact information for Charlie Roth of the *Jewish Post*. They dialed the telephone number and handed the phone to Eliezer, who said, "Hello, I am Eliezer, the Servant of the Lord. I am here in Bellevue hospital for passing out leaflets in front of Congregation Emanu-El. Until now I have not spoken because it was *yontif* (a holy day), but now that *yontif* is over I have had them call your number. Would you please come and get me?"

Charlie had no idea who this man was or any idea as to how he had gotten his number, but he got on his Vespa scooter and went over to Bellevue hospital to pick him up. There, Charlie listened to Eliezer's story then took him home to his apartment and fed him. After that, Eliezer left.

Several days later, on Yom Kippur, he showed up again, this time in front of the Society for the Advancement of Judaism, the Reconstructionist synagogue. Again, he handed someone a leaflet and they took it inside to show the rabbi. This time the rabbi was Mordechai Kaplan, the founder of Reconstructionism. "Should we call the police?" asked the person who presented the leaflet to the rabbi.

"No, no," he answered. "Please ask this gentleman to come in and read his pamphlet from the pulpit." But when they asked Eliezer to read the material from the pulpit, he said, "That is not what God asked me to do. You read it from the pulpit if you want."

I was told that after this event he left New York and went back to Chicago, where he lived. At that time, my sister was living in Chicago and I asked her if, by chance, she knew Eliezer, because his family name was Schachter, our own family name. "Eliezer! He is our roofer, our tinsmith," she said. I asked her to arrange a meeting with him the next time I was in Chicago, so I could speak with him. My sister agreed.

So the next time I was in Chicago I drove to his address, and his mother let me in. Immediately I saw Eliezer standing over a homeless person whom he had just fed, and his mother, one of those wonderful holy ladies, sweet and pious, said to me, "My *kusher zin*, my kosher son, he is such a kind person." Then Eliezer turned to me and said, "You wait for me. I have to feed this person." When he finished with the man, he came over to me. "Give him ten dollars," Eliezer instructed me. What was I going to do, argue with him? I gave the man ten dollars, and then Eliezer sat down with me to find out what I wanted. I asked him if he would be willing to come and speak to some friends of mine. He agreed.

When he visited we asked him a few questions. "How did this happen to you?" someone asked.

"One day, God spoke to me and said, 'Take down this dictation.' So I took down the dictation. Then God said, 'I want you to publicize this.' 'Well,' I said, 'you wanted me take down the dictation, I took down the dictation; more I can't do right now.' The next day I got to work and someone said to me, 'Eliezer, I hear you need some typing done.' So I realized I was trapped, and I gave her the dictation. On the next day she brought it back to me typed out. Just after that, another acquaintance came to me and said, 'I have a mimeograph machine and I understand that you need one.' I realized that there was no avoiding this, and I have been doing this work ever since."

"What is it like when God talks to you?" someone asked Eliezer.

"That is what every psychologist wants to know," he replied.

"How do you know it's God and not the devil?" someone else asked.

"That's what every judge wants to know," he replied. He didn't answer any questions after that.

Was he a prophet? What can I say? He was a servant of the Lord and I really loved him in his humility and the way in which he saw himself as fully an instrument of God.

Preface ☐

Do the Hebrew prophets matter? This is the first question you must ask yourself when deciding whether or not to read this book. If you say "no," then there is no reason to proceed. If you say "yes," you must then ask what your "yes" means.

Saying "no" to the prophets relegates them to the dustbin of history; affirming that there is nothing in their lives that speaks to your life, and therefore no reason to bother with them at all. While this is a legitimate position to take, it is also one I find less than convincing. For me the prophets are not only valuable, but critical. Their lives not only relate to mine; they challenge mine. The prophets reflected God's way in their own lives; that is, they stood in direct relation to God, experienced the essence of living in tune with godliness. They then spoke their truth, and in so doing allow me to see more clearly the truth and falsehood of my own experience.

Saying "yes" to the prophets places you in direct conversation with them. It allows the prophets to speak directly to you about your life right here, right now. This is the way the prophets' contemporaries heard them. This is the way the prophets themselves expected to be heard. And this is the primary way they can continue to be relevant to you.

In his book *The Prophetic Faith,* Martin Buber said the prophet and his audience have a symbiotic relationship. The prophet needs to be heard, and the people need to be addressed. The prophet's task is to confront you with a choice, with the necessity of making a decision regarding the quality of your life, both personal and communal. The future is fluid, not fixed. It is created by choices made in the present. Choose one way and your future is bleak; choose another and your future is bright. Everything depends on the choice you make in the present moment. The prophets simply bring the ultimate choice into focus: Do you choose for God and godliness, or do you choose for self and selfishness?

Because the choice is yours, the future is yours as well. And because the prophet reminds you that you have the power to choose differently this moment than you did in the past, the prophet reminds you of the power of *teshuvah*. While conventionally understood as "repentance," *teshuvah* literally means "to turn," and refers to your innate ability to turn from ignorance to truth, from injustice to justice, from despair to joy. It is your capacity to turn from the wrong path to the right path that makes the prophets relevant to your life.

Thousands of years after they spoke, their words still have the power to place the ultimate choice before you, but only if you place yourself in the audience. This is the approach I take in this book. I want you to feel directly addressed by the words of the prophet, and thereby confronted by the need to choose.

I wrote this book because I believe that the prophets are speaking to you and me about things we desperately need to hear and to know. I believe that the prophets are giving voice to eternal principles, but voice alone is not enough. You have to dare to hear what the prophet dares to speak, and then you must dare to respond to what you hear in the immediacy of your own life.

The prophets are speaking to you, though not to you alone. They need you to listen as only you can; to listen with ears attuned to your life and your situation so you might hear what it is you need to hear in this moment in order to decide how you must engage this moment. And because each moment is fresh, and each decision new, you will find yourself returning to the words of the prophets over and over again. Keep this book on your desk or by your bedside. At least once each day, pick it up and read a section or two at random. Don't rush to my comments right away. Put the book down and listen to what you have just read. What is the prophet saying to you? Then go to my notes and see if they enrich your own response to the prophet's words. Where they do, let them into your listening. Where they do not, simply acknowledge that there are many layers to these teachings, and that you are looking for your own understanding and should not be distracted by mine.

To help with this kind of listening, I do not follow the convention of offering separate chapters on each prophet. Instead, I divide the book into four main sections, and invite a number of prophets to speak in each. The first section deals with the nature of the prophetic mission. The second, third, and fourth sections deal with the three acts of *teshuvah* the prophets call you to make in your life: from ignorance to truth, and seeing that God is all in all; from injustice to justice, and engaging life from a sense of holiness and wholeness that sees all beings as manifestations of the One Being; and from despair to joy, or what you might call salvation, that sense of freedom and ease that arises when you know God and act in a godly way. Juxtaposing prophets in this way breaks down their historical context and highlights the immediacy of their message. In this book it doesn't matter that Amos is speaking in the third century while Jeremiah is speaking in the eighth century. They are both speaking to you right now. Listen well, and turn.

Acknowledgments ☐

This was not a book I had to write; it was a book that had to be written. The idea for this book came from my friend, colleague, and teacher, Andrew Harvey, the editor of this series of books from SkyLight Paths. We were in Tucson, Arizona, and Andrew heard me speak on the relevance of the Hebrew prophets. My comments sparked the idea for a book of teachings from the Hebrew prophets that would speak directly to contemporary readers. He asked me to take on the task. I am grateful to him for the opportunity to sharpen my own appreciation of these extraordinary human beings, and to share my understanding of them with you.

The clarity of that understanding owes a great deal to my editor, Emily Wichland, who kneaded the raw dough of my writing into this rich loaf of prophetic teaching. Thanks, too, goes to Jon Sweeney of SkyLight Paths, who was gracious enough to invite me to produce a second volume for his masterful Illuminations series.

This book is dedicated to the memory of Teresina Havens, my first spiritual guide and mentor.

A Note on Translation: The Nature of God and the Power of Prophecy ☐

Translation is always a matter of interpretation. Every language is too rich and too nuanced to be directly translatable into another. The translator has to get inside the mind of the author to find just the right word to convey what is found in that mind. But in this case there is no "getting inside the mind of the author"; there is only getting inside the mind of the translator trying to make sense of the text. What you will read on these pages is not what the prophets wrote, but what I hear and understand when I read them.

Because of this, it is often helpful to compare my translations with more conventional readings. I suggest you consult the New Revised Standard Version of the Bible, the Jerusalem Bible, and even Eugene H. Peterson's Message Bible, along with the fine Hebrew/English Bibles published by Artscroll and the Jewish Publication Society. In this way, you will come to understand even more clearly what I hear in the words of these spiritual giants, and be better able to hear their message for yourself as well.

I have striven for a dramatic reading of the prophets—a reading that is clearly interpretive and driven by both the richness of contemporary American English and my own spiritual grasp of what the prophets are saying to us in our day. This is not the only way to read these prophets, but it is a powerful one.

There are two aspects to this translation of the Hebrew prophets that makes this book unique: the use of the second person singular pronoun *you* in place of the name of specific peoples or groups, and my rendering of *YHVH*, conventionally translated as Lord, as *The One Who Is*. Let me take a moment to explain each of these departures.

The prophets were speaking to specific people at specific points in history. Listening to the prophets, these people experienced themselves as being directly addressed by God: Choose between truth and ignorance, justice and injustice, joy and despair. I want you to experience the prophetic utterance in a similar manner. God is speaking to you no less than the ancients. You, no less than they, are being asked to choose. To emphasize the personal nature of the prophetic address, I use the word *you* where the original addresses specific peoples. My intent is to place you in the prophet's audience, to help you feel challenged to evaluate your life in light of the prophet's teaching. While this is a departure from conventional translation, it is the best way I know to honor the true nature of the prophet's address.

An equally radical choice is made regarding the translation of the ineffable Name of God. While we are used to seeing *YHVH* rendered as Lord, this tells us nothing of the nature of the One Who speaks through the prophets.

According to historical records, the Tetragrammaton (the four-lettered Name of God) was originally spoken aloud. Beginning in the third century B.C.E., however, the name *YHVH* was written but no longer read aloud, replaced instead by *Adonai*, Lord. This is still how Jews read the Name today. In the Middle Ages, Christian clerics took the Hebrew vowels constituting *Adonai* and assigned them to the four Hebrew consonants of *YHVH*, eventually resulting in the word *Jehovah*. *Jehovah* and *Lord* are euphemisms, however, and tell you nothing about the nature of God, whereas the original Hebrew *YHVH* reveals the true essence of God.

YHVH is derived from the Hebrew verb *to be.* God is what is. God is not a being, or even the Supreme Being, but Being itself. God is the Source and Substance of all that was, is, and ever will be. God is all that is, and it is for this reason that I choose to translate *YHVH* not as Lord but as *The One Who Is.*

I am a nondualist. I believe that God is all that is, even as God is greater than all that is. I believe that your relationship with God is analogous to the relationship of a wave to the ocean. The wave is not other than the ocean, and yet the ocean is so much more than the wave. God does not dwell in you, above you, outside of you—God is you. When you realize your true relationship with God, you feel connected to all reality and discover that you are connected to all beings in, with, and as God. This awakening compels you to act justly, compassionately, and humbly: the very ideals the prophets so highly value.

When the prophet speaks to you in the voice of God, you are hearing the deepest truths of your own being echoed in their words. It is as if your greater self, the self aware of itself as one with God, were addressing your smaller self, the ego that, while also a manifestation of God, insists that it is other than God. It is the ego that sees the world as an arena of competing beings vying for the biggest piece of a fixed pie. It is the ego that shifts from self to selfishness, and engages in unjust, cruel, and exploitative behavior. It is the ego that needs to hear the prophetic challenge; it is the ego that needs to turn. And when it does, it turns toward its greater self and reconnects with God and engages creation justly, lovingly, and humbly.

Given the nonduality of God, and Isaiah's bold affirmation of this—I create light and dark, good and evil; I the One Who Is, do all these things (Isaiah 45:7)—you might wonder why it matters to God that you choose ignorance over truth, justice over injustice, joy over despair. It doesn't matter to God. It matters to you and the quality of life you experience in the relative world of time and space.

Think of it this way: The ocean manifests an infinite number of waves. It is its nature to do so. It is not a matter of choice. It is what it is to be an ocean. The ocean also has a current. This too is not a matter of choice; it simply is what is. Now, God manifests beings the way the ocean raises waves. It is what God does. And God has a current: justice, compassion, and humility celebrated by the prophets. Unlike waves, however, you have a choice to flow with the current or against it. It is not that God will punish you if you choose to go against the current of godliness; it is that

God cannot support you when you do so. As with the ocean, you can swim against the current, but doing so will exhaust you and you will drown. Swimming with the current, on the other hand, allows the ocean to sustain you, to carry you, to make it possible for you to live long and prosper. It is the same with God. Act violently and violence will destroy you. Act kindly and compassion will sustain you. The prophets are calling you to swim with the current, to live in sync with the divine principles of truth, justice, compassion, and humility, and in so doing experience the joy of being buoyed by God.

My theology may not mesh with yours, and you are free to understand God as you wish. All I suggest to you is this: However you choose to envision God, see yourself addressed by God in these pages, and allow yourself to turn from self to God and from selfishness to godliness, and in this way abandon the idolatry that keeps you from discovering your connection with the One Who Is.

Introduction □

It's the role of the prophet to keep people free for God.... It's the responsibility of the prophet to keep God free for the people.

—Richard Rohr

What does it mean to be free for God? If you want to understand the prophets of the Hebrew Bible and how their teachings can transform your life, you must be able to answer this question. Being free for God means engaging each moment uncluttered by the psychological and spiritual baggage of the past. It means encountering God, nature, and everyone you meet from a place of radical not-knowing. It means putting aside the idolatries that pass for truth in your life, and learning to live without surety, certainty, and rationalization. It means standing naked before the mirror of Truth and seeing all your imperfections, and not being quite clear as to whether they are imperfections or not. It means living without a net. The prophets' chief task is to tear down the safety nets we set up for ourselves, and then to challenge us to live in radical freedom, knowing that in doing so we are also choosing radical insecurity.

Radical insecurity is the way of God: "The One Who Is said to Avram, 'Go forth from your land, away from your people, out of your father's house, to the land that I will let you see'" (Genesis 12:1). This is God's call to you as well: Free yourself from the influences of nationalism, ethnicity, and parental bias, and then see the world as it is: a manifestation of the One Who Is. How do you do this? The Hebrew text tells us, for the English "Go forth" is in Hebrew *lech lecha,* literally "Go into yourself." God calls you to turn from the small self *(mochin d'katnut),* which worships the gods of nation, tribe, race, and ancestors, to your greater self *(mochin d'gadlut),* which worships God alone. Living without the foundation—however false—of nationality, ethnicity, race, and ancestral ties is frightening. It means living without a fixed identity. Yet this is exactly what God is calling you to do. Your true identity is God, and God is unconditioned, new, and fresh each moment.

Few people dare to live this way. To counter God's call to unconditionality, you construct all sorts of nets to keep yourself from falling into the radical freedom of unknowing and uncertainty that is key to seeing the world as God in God. These nets are the idols you worship—the work of your imagination that bolsters your sense of separation from God, alienation from life, and estrangement from your greater self. You worship the idols of the small self that subtly maintain the illusion that this self is all of you, and that you are other than the world and the One Who manifests it.

Idols are false gods because they do not reveal the true nature of God as all in all. Idols speak to the small self and offer it a sense of meaning and purpose that blinds it to the deeper meaning and purpose of life that only the greater self can fathom. When the prophets call you an idolater, do not dismiss the charge saying, "I worship no images," but know they are challenging you to give up the worship of the small self and those fantasies that proclaim it sovereign.

I learned this truth most memorably during my freshman year at the University of Massachusetts in Amherst. In 1969, I organized a "Breathe-In," a daylong meditation retreat for students and faculty exhausted by the heated rhetoric and violence that had shut down the campus after revelations about U.S. bombing raids in Cambodia. I fancied myself a student of Zen Buddhism at the time, having read lots of books on the subject, and having spent a day with Phillip Kapleau Roshi from the First Zen Institute in Rochester, New York.

Not yet ready to proclaim myself a meditation master, I found a professor in the English Department willing to take on that role and lead the retreat. We assembled early on a Wednesday morning. There must have been 250 of us dressed in loose clothing and sitting on cushions and chairs. Those in chairs sat in the back half of the lecture hall I had reserved. Those on cushions sat in the front. I was in the front. I was very serious.

With the ringing of the meditation bell, the room fell silent. Soft breathing and an occasional cough were the only sounds breaking the silence. Sitting crossed-legged, my eyes open and unfocused, resting my gaze about eighteen inches in front of me, I became aware of an elderly woman ("elderly" because I was nineteen; she was only sixty) sitting one row in front of me, slightly to my right. She was thin, gray-haired, and a bit wild looking. And she moved.

Moving in meditation is a cardinal sin, but this old woman not only shifted on her cushion, she put it under her head and lay down to sleep. Unbelievable! I spent the next forty-five minutes focused solely on this sleeping old lady, contrasting her lack of discipline with my finely tuned loyalty to Zen form and formulae. When the bell rang, signaling the end of our first sitting session, the old woman awoke, sat up, turned to face me, and said, "Sometimes you just have to sleep."

This was my introduction to my first guru. Her name was Teresina Havens. She was a retired professor of religion, and lived with her husband, Joe, off the grid in the forests of Shutesbury, Massachusetts. We talked during every break, and by the end of the day we had agreed to meet one afternoon each week to study and meditate together. Most of our time was spent studying Sanskrit and the Bhagavad Gita. Part of every visit was devoted to eating things in the forest that Terry insisted were edible, but that tasted otherwise. All I learned from these culinary exercises was never to walk in the woods without salt; lots of salt. Sometimes our conversations turned to things biblical, often to the prophets.

"The Hebrew prophets are unique in the history of religion," she told me one autumn afternoon. "Where most spiritual books tend to uplift the reader, the books of the prophets tear them down. They are, to use Christian terminology, masters of the Via Negativa."

The Via Negativa, the Negative Way, is the way of stripping away what we think we know in order to come to the Truth. It is the Hindu *Neti Neti,* "Not this, not that," that denies absolute reality to anything we can imagine. It is Lao Tzu writing in the *Tao te Ching,* "The Tao that can be named (literally *tao*-ed) is not the Eternal Tao." It is the unnamed and unnamable God of Moses.

Terry continued, "When Moses meets God at the Burning Bush and asks God to reveal the divine Name, what Name does God offer?" She looked at me intently, expecting me to know something that I knew I didn't know. No matter what I said, I knew it wasn't going to be enough.

"God says *Ehyeh asher Ehyeh,*" I said, "I am what I am."

"Not at all," Terry said. "'I am what I am' limits God to one mode of being. God is then static, unchanging, and, from the human point of view, irrelevant. But that is not how God refers to God. God says *Ehyeh asher Ehyeh,* not 'I am what I am" but 'I shall be what I shall be,' meaning you cannot limit God to a name or a form. God is whatever God decides to be. God is not unchanging; God is change itself. God is always surprising us, but the only way we can be surprised by God is if we admit fully that we have no idea what God is. Do you understand?"

This was one of those moments when a bit of honesty could have brought on a lot of wisdom. I should have said, "No, I don't understand." Instead I smiled and said, "Sure, I understand." Terry knew I was lying, but let me eat the empty calories of ignorance rather than waste a bit of wisdom on someone too scared to admit to not knowing.

"Religion is the way we humans avoid having to be surprised by God," she said. "We invent a god who delights in form, and then worship the form in hopes of pleasing the god. The prophets knew this— all prophets know this. That is why they keep reminding us that God doesn't care about ritual. The prophets of the Bible are forever challenging the easy notion that God wants sacrifices and ceremony, when in fact all God wants is the heart; a heart attuned to justice, compassion, and humility.

"The question is: Can you live without form? Can you approach God without the theories and ideologies of religion? Can you take off your shoes as Moses does when meeting God at the Burning Bush, and just be present to the One Who Is Present? Can you," she repeated herself for emphasis, "live without form?"

Smart-ass student of Zen that I was, I quoted the *Heart Sutra* to her, "Form is emptiness, emptiness is form." Terry just stared at me, amazed at my own foolishness. "When you really know what that means," she said sternly, "you may say it again. Until then be quiet." She then kicked over a stone, scraped something green off the bottom of it, and handed it me. "Here," she said, "eat this." I had forgotten the salt.

Was I wrong to point out a connection between the *Heart Sutra* and the heart of the prophetic message? No, just premature. In Jewish terms, "Form is emptiness, emptiness is form" means that God is both the One and the Many, the Absolute and the Relative. The prophets are not telling us to live without form, but to live our forms from a deep understanding of emptiness. That is to say use form but do not abuse form. Or use form but do not be used by it.

Now apply this to God's call to Avram. Can you use your nationality, ethnicity, race, and ancestral ties without being used by them? Can you draw upon these things without worshiping them? Can you see them as windows into the world rather than funhouse mirrors distorting your view of the world by reflecting back to you a distorted view of yourself?

This is what God calls you to do; this is what the prophets challenge you to do: Turn inward, free yourself of the distortions you worship, and engage the world justly, kindly, and simply.

This is not the totality of what the prophets have to say, but it is at the core. The relentless prophetic attack on form for form's sake, on ritual as a way of controlling God, on a theology that is at root manipulative, reducing God to a puppet pulled by priestly strings, is in effect an attack on your own egocentric thinking. Freeing God from theology and ritual is what Richard Rohr calls keeping God free for the people. Freeing yourself from manipulative thinking is what he calls keeping the people free for

God. Both are linked to the prophets' passionate attack on idolatry and the ignorance, injustice, and despair idolatry carries with it.

Idolatry is the worship of false gods, gods that cannot save you. Being saved means being awake to your true nature as God manifest in your particular time and place. Waking to this truth happens when you turn from the idols and the ignorance, injustice, and despair that support them, meet the One Who Is, and engage life with truth, justice, and joy.

What your idols share with their ancient carved and graven counterparts is this: They deplete your freedom and rob you of choice. You may not call the false gods of your life *gods*, but they are gods nonetheless. Racism, sexism, homophobia, xenophobia, and anti-Semitism are modern gods of chaos and violence that steal your ability to see people as individuals, and to treat them justly and kindly. Avarice, workaholism, self-loathing, and conceit are gods of inner turmoil that rob you of compassion. Drugs, sex, alcohol, and the rest of modernity's addictions are all gods of despair that make joy and freedom impossible.

You may not worship all or even any of these gods, but you have your own and they are no less false and deadly. When you read the prophets attacking idolatry, do not imagine that they are speaking to someone else. Denial is the food of the false gods. It is what sustains them and their power over you. Denial clouds your mind from the truth of the prophet's claim that you are an idolater. Listen to the prophets and let the fog of denial burn away before the heat of their stinging rebuke. Only when you see the idols you worship are you capable of freeing yourself from them.

> We are witnessing today an historical phenomenon of crucial importance: the almost complete conquest of industrial society by a new paganism.… This new idolatry … is not the worship of certain gods instead of others, or of one god instead of many. It is a human attitude, that of the reification of all that is alive. It is a man's submission to things, his self-negation as a living, open, ego-transcending being. Idols are gods that do not liberate; in worshipping idols, man makes himself a prisoner and renounces liberation. Idols are gods that do not live; in worshipping idols, man himself is deadened.[1]

The new paganism is the worship of things. This is what psychologist Erich Fromm calls the Way of Having. The Way of Having seeks to fill the void in our lives with the ownership of things. The problem is, of course, that the pleasure we obtain from ownership is fleeting, and as it passes we are driven to find more things to own.

The opposite of the Way of Having is the Way of Being. The Way of Being is rooted not in what you own but in who you are, and who you are is the image of God (Genesis 1:27). Your worth is rooted in your very existence. You may be more or less wealthy, intelligent, successful, and the like, but none of this affects your essential value as a human being. You are valuable because you are an image of God, a manifestation of the Divine in your particular time and place. You are an extension of God the way a wave is an extension of the ocean, and a branch is an extension of a tree.

The Way of Being is the Way of God. This is especially clear when we recall the Hebrew name of God, YHVH, and God's self-definition in Exodus 3:14, *Ehyeh asher Ehyeh,* which is composed of variations of the Hebrew verb "to be." God is Being, the One Who Is all that is.

To participate in Being you must simply be. Having, owning, coveting, hoarding, and the like do not enhance your being at all. Yet it is just this that drives you.

> Today's idols are the objects of a systematically cultivated greed: for money, power, lust, glory, food, and drink. Man worships the means and ends of this greed: production, consumption, military might, business, and the state. The stronger he makes his idols, the poorer he becomes, and the emptier he feels. Instead of joy, he seeks thrill; instead of life, he loves a mechanized world of gadgets; instead of growth, he seeks wealth; instead of being, he is interested in having and using. As a result, modern man has lost any comprehensive system of values except those idolatrous ones; he is anxious, depressed, hopeless, and ready to risk nuclear self-destruction because life has ceased to make sense, to be interesting, and to give joy.[2]

Joy, on the other hand, is precisely what the prophets promise: "Then will the young women rejoice in the dance, both young men and old together: for I will turn their mourning into joy" (Jeremiah 31:13); "With joy you will draw water" (Isaiah 12:3); God calls Jerusalem "the city of My joy" (Jeremiah 49:25). Joy is the quality of freedom, the quality of being rather than having. When the prophets rant against idolatry, they are not speaking about ancient fools throwing themselves on the ground in praise of wooden dolls; they are speaking of timeless foolishness that places power in the work of your hands rather than the quality of your relationships.

> God, originally a symbol for the highest value that we can experience within us, becomes, in the having mode, an idol. In the prophetic concept, an idol is a thing that we ourselves make and project our own powers into, thus impoverishing ourselves. We then submit to our creation and by our submission we are in touch with ourselves in an alienated form. While I can *have* the idol because it is a thing, by my submission to it, *it,* simultaneously, has *me.*[3]

Having and being had is, for the prophets, the great sin. The God of the prophets cannot be had, and therefore cannot have you. The God of the prophets is the opposite of an idol. From the second of the Ten Commandments to the prophets themselves, any god that can be fashioned as an image is not the eternal God.

> Faith, in the having mode, is a crutch for those who want to be certain, those who want an answer to life without daring to search for it themselves. In the being mode faith is an entirely different phenomenon…. Faith, in the being mode, is not, in the first place, a belief in certain ideas (although it may be that, too) but an inner orientation, an *attitude.* It would be better to say that one *is in* faith than that one *has* faith.[4]

The prophets' challenge is to accept the freedom of uncertainty, insecurity, and not-knowing. Their way is the way of radical freedom, and they know that failure to be free can only result in enslavement to self and selfishness, and eventually exile from all that is meaningful and joyous in life.

> These revolutionary thinkers, the Hebrew prophets, renewed the vision of human freedom—of being unfettered of things—and the protest against submitting to idols—the work of the people's own hands. They were uncompromising and predicted that the people would have to be expelled from the land again if they became incestuously fixated to it and incapable of living in it as free people—that is, not able to live in it without losing themselves in it. To the prophets the expulsion from the land was a tragedy, but the only way to final liberation; the new desert was to last not one but for many generations. Even while predicting the new desert, the prophets were sustaining the faith of the Jews, and eventually of the whole human race, by the Messianic vision that promised peace and abundance without requiring the expulsion or extermination of the land's old inhabitants.[5]

A life of having is a life of being had. A life of being is a life of freedom. The "having life" is authoritarian and based on the false notion that you are other than the One Who Is. Alienated from God, you are forced to search for salvation, your sense of wholeness, by submitting yourself to externals. The "being life" is liberating and rooted in your unity with God as the One Who Is all things. Finding refuge in God, you are free from externals, you lack nothing, need little, and fear no one.

The ultimate gift of this life of being is peace. Peace means far more to the prophets than the absence of war, though that would be no mean accomplishment. Peace, in Hebrew *shalom*, comes from the root *s-l-m*, which means "wholeness." Peace is the sense of wholeness and completeness that arises when we realize the interconnectedness of all things. Peace need not end all conflict. As long as there are people with egos, there will be competing needs, visions, and values. Peace means that we will see others as partners in a dance rather than enemies at war. Each will learn to push against the other to help clarify and enhance the other's sense of justice and mercy.

This is not a return to some pristine state of human existence; this is the evolution of human consciousness to a higher level of knowing. There is a tendency among some who speculate on these issues to imagine that the past was better than the future. They posit a Golden Age from which we have fallen and toward which we strive to return. In biblical terms, we could speak of this Golden Age as the Garden of Eden. The exile of Adam and Eve from Eden is often referred to as the Fall of Humankind. Judaism, however, never speaks of it this way.

The expulsion from Eden was a necessary step in the evolution of human consciousness from the pre-personal to the transpersonal. Before eating of the fruit of the Tree of Knowledge of Good and Evil, Adam and Eve were naked and unashamed. That is to say, they were without egos, without self-consciousness. Their lack of shame was due not to their acceptance of their nakedness but to their obliviousness to it.

When they eat of the Tree and their eyes are open—that is, when they reach a level of awareness that allows them to see opposites such as good and evil—they are aware of themselves as self and other. This low level of self-awareness is accompanied by a sense of shame; not shame in a moral sense, but shame meaning an alienating sense of self-consciousness. It is this alone that exiles them from the Garden. Eden is no place for self.

We are used to thinking of their act of eating the fruit as a sin. This is not what the Torah says. Nowhere does the Torah use the word *sin* to refer to this action. It was an act of disobedience, but disobedience is part of the evolution of consciousness. The self emerges as a self by distinguishing itself from other selves. From the perspective of others, this may be an act of disobedience, but from the perspective of the self it is a bold move toward wisdom.

There are consequences to this move, what the Bible calls a curse. What is the curse? Conflict and struggle. Earthling *(adam)* and earth *(adamah)* are in conflict; man, woman, and nature are in conflict; man and woman are in conflict; even women and their natural function as bearers of children is seen as a struggle. Struggle and conflict are natural to free beings, natural but not inevitable. What is inevitable is a period of struggle as the newly emerging self begins the long evolutionary quest toward self-transcendence.

> Man has to experience himself as a stranger in the world, as estranged from himself and from nature, in order to be able to become one again with himself, with his fellow man, and with nature. He has to experience the split between himself as subject and object as the condition for overcoming this very split. His first sin, disobedience, is the first act of freedom; it is the beginning of human history. It is in history that man develops, evolves, and emerges. He develops his reason and his capacity to love. He creates himself in the historical process which began with his first act of freedom, which is the freedom to disobey, to say "No."[6]

But is this evolution from pre-personal to transpersonal guaranteed? Not at all. The Bible is a panorama of the rise and fall of human consciousness. Over and again we strive for justice and loving our neighbor only to fall back on violence and cruelty toward those neighbors. Where is God in all of this?

God isn't in this process; the process is in God. The Bible is telling us how God evolves beings capable of knowing God as other, and ultimately as one. You are one of those beings. Yet not all people arrive at this state of knowing at the same time. Some are ahead and some behind. The prophets of all faiths are the vanguard. They are the few who see what awaits the many when they learn to transcend the small self and see reality for what it is: a manifestation of God. This is the wave waking up to its oceanic essence.

The prophets remind you of your greater self, and the spiritual ideals that self embodies. They show you the consequences of your actions when you violate those ideals, and challenge you every time you choose those ideal-violating actions. Or, to put it very simply: The prophets push you from having to being, from idolatry to freedom.

Freedom, however, is not what you naturally crave. It seems that soon after your first act of disobedience, soon after you realize you have the capacity to say "no," you flee from the consequences of freedom and seek to hide behind strong leaders to whom you say "yes." This is the story of the prophet Samuel anointing Saul as the first king of Israel.

> All the elders of Israel came together and met with Samuel saying, "You are old, and your sons are wicked; give us a king like those of other nations" (1 Samuel 8:5).... Samuel resisted—this was not what God wanted from them—so he prayed to God for guidance. God said to Samuel, "Do as they request for it is not you they are rejecting but Me ... they are forsaking Me and worshiping the gods of others ... So give them their king, but warn them of kingship and the madness they are bringing upon themselves" (1 Samuel 8:6–9).

God, the unconditioned and unconditionable, was to rule over the people. That is to say, freedom was to be their ideal. By crowning a king, they fled from freedom into the slavery of worshiping humans and the things of human hands. Samuel warned the people, but they did not care. Freedom then as now is too frightening for many of us to imagine, let alone handle for ourselves.

Nor do you stop at kings. You submit to priests and Levites, magicians and shamans. You look everywhere for a god who will save you from the freedom with which you are destined to wrestle. And when your hiding becomes so great as to allow you to forget your true mission as a free being, a prophet arises to remind you.

The mission of the prophet is to push you out of one hideout after another. Wherever you hide, the prophet pulls back the curtain of delusion and demands that you look at your ignorance and the consequences of it.

Why doesn't God simply return you to freedom? Because that would be to return you to the pre-personal infancy of the original Garden. You need to work out your own salvation by learning how to actualize freedom in the world of competing selves. You need to move from the pre-personal through the personal in order to arrive at the salvation that is the transpersonal.

Man's first act of freedom is an act of disobedience; by this act he transcends his original oneness with nature, he becomes aware of himself and of his neighbor and of their estrangement. In the historical process, man creates himself. He grows in self-awareness, in love, in justice, and when he has reached the aim of the full grasp of the world by his own power of reason and love, he has become one again, he has undone the original "sin," he has returned to Paradise, but on the new level of human individualization and independence.... This completion of his self-creation, the end of the history of strife and conflict and the beginning of a new history of harmony and union, is called "messianic time," "the end of days," etc.[7]

While in general agreement on this point from Fromm, I would go a bit further. It is not simply that you have reached a level of healthy independence, but that you have come to see yourself as interdependent with all beings. The messianic time is not simply a time of self-realization, but of Self-realization. That is to say, the pre-personal self of the Garden of Eden has passed through the self-conscious stage of individuation to realize the transpersonal stage of seeing oneself as a part of the whole and no longer apart from it. This is the meaning of *shalom/shalem*, peace as wholeness and harmony.

The prophetic call, the prophetic vision, the prophetic hope for humankind is the fulfillment of the promise that came with that first "no"; the promise of a greater "yes." As you shall see, the images the prophets offer of this messianic time are images of renewed harmony and unity, a unity that does not erase diversity, but embraces it in a new earthly paradise of beings aligned with the One Who Is All.

In order to have peace, man must find "atonement"; peace is the result of a transformation of man in which union has replaced alienation. Thus the idea of peace, in the prophetic view, cannot be separated from the idea of man's realization of his humanity. Peace is more than a condition of no war; it is harmony and union between men, it is the overcoming of separateness and alienation.... The prophetic concept of peace transcends the realm of human relations; the new

> harmony is also between man and nature ... man is not threatened by
> nature and determined to dominate it: he becomes natural, and
> nature becomes human. He and nature cease to be opponents and
> become one. Man is at home in the natural world. This is peace in
> the prophetic sense.[8]

You might think that nothing could be more natural to you than this
desire to move forward into freedom, and yet, nothing could be further
from the truth.

> Not to move forward, to stay where we are, to regress, in other words
> to rely on what we have, is very tempting, for what we have, we
> know; we can hold onto it, feel secure in it. We fear, and consequently
> avoid, taking a step into the unknown, the uncertain; for, indeed,
> while the step may appear risky to us after we have taken it, before
> we take that step the new aspects beyond it appear very risky, and
> hence frightening. Only the old, the tried, is safe; or so it seems. Every
> new step contains the danger of failure, and that is one of the reasons
> people are so afraid of freedom.[9]

The prophets are challenging you to say "no" to one of your most
basic instincts, the instinct to stay put. To stay put is to allow yourself to
become static, unchanging, and rigid. It is to reject God's call to move
inward and free yourself from the idols that bind, blind, and condition
you. It is to invest absolute power in *mochin d'katnut,* the narrow mind or
small self of ego. This is the opposite of what life is about, and a life lived
in such a way leaves you feeling alienated from God who is *Ehyeh asher
Ehyeh,* the ever-changing reality of this and every moment.

The prophets speak to you from *mochin d'gadlut,* the spacious mind,
the greater self that knows it is one with God and who acts in a godly way,
engaging each moment with justice, kindness, and humility. If you listen
to what they say from the same mindset with which they say it, you will
turn from ignorance to truth, from injustice to justice, from despair to
joy, and in so turning discover the truth of who you are: a unique wave ris-
ing from, in, and as the ocean of God.

Brief Biographies of the Hebrew Prophets ▢

Amos

The earliest of the literary prophets, those whose words are found in books bearing their names, Amos was a mid–eighth century B.C.E. Judean rancher and farmer, raising livestock and growing fruit trees in Tekoa (Amos 7:14). Called by God to leave Judea for the Northern Kingdom of Israel, Amos verbally attacks the sacrificial cult of Beth-El with its self-assured magic, and offers instead a universal vision of the Divine, rooted in justice. He calls the priests, the politicians, and the general populace to a new way of life before their old ways force them into exile.

"Your offerings disgust Me, and I am not flattered by your gatherings ... Disperse your choirs and musicians; I am deaf to them all. Rather, let justice bubble up like a fresh spring, and righteousness like a mighty stream" (Amos 5:21–24). Humanity's task, Amos teaches, is to "despise evil and love good, and establish justice in the gate" (Amos 5:15).

Troubled by this reformer, Amaziah, a priest of Beth-El, denounces Amos to King Jeroboam II. While prophesying the death of the king, Amos returns to the Southern Kingdom of Judea, where his book is most likely written.

Elijah

Elijah lived during the reign of King Ahab of Israel and his son Ahaziah (ninth century B.C.E.). His central concern is the influence of the god Baal and his priests. Brought into prominence by Jezebel, King Ahab's Phoenician wife, Baal and his consort Astarte rival YHVH for the loyalty of the people. Elijah challenges the priests of Baal to a contest at Mount

Carmel (1 Kings 18:16ff.) in the sight of representatives from all over Israel.

Elijah demands that the Israelites choose between YHVH and Baal, but they remain silent. Elijah then challenges the priests of Baal to a duel. He and they will each slay a bull and prepare it as a burnt offering, but no fire is to be kindled. Rather, the 450 priests of Baal will call out to their god and, if the fire of their altar ignites they will win and their god will be acknowledged as God. But if not, Elijah will invoke YHVH and the people will see what is true about God and gods.

The priests of Baal raise up a great noise and dance mightily to draw down the attention and the fire of Baal, but to no avail. Elijah then gathers the Israelites to him; builds an altar of twelve stones, signifying the twelve tribes of Israel; kills his bull; and calls to God, "Answer me, YHVH, answer me! And thereby let this people know that You, YHVH, are God" (1 Kings 18:37). Fire from heaven consumes both the bull and the altar, and the people fall on their faces, shouting, "YHVH is God! YHVH is God!" (1 Kings 18:39). Using their frenzy to his advantage, Elijah orders the people to capture the priests of Baal and take them to the river at Kishon, where he slaughters them all.

Elijah himself never dies. Rather, he is taken up to heaven in a chariot of fire drawn by horses of flame (2 Kings 2). Because of this, legends grow up around Elijah. He is said to appear to people in need, offering help and comfort. The prophet Malachi reveals that it will be Elijah who will return to earth to announce the end times (Malachi 3:23).

Elijah is invoked during the Hebrew grace after meals: "The Merciful One will send us Elijah the prophet, may he be remembered for the good, and he will bring us good news, comfort, and consolation"; and at the annual Passover Seder where a fifth cup of wine, called Elijah's Cup, is filled and the prophet is invited to enter the home to drink with the family and bring them news of peace.

Elisha

Elijah's disciple, aide, and successor, Elisha continued his master's struggle with Ahab and his descendents, going as far as to have one of his own disciples anoint Jehu king as rival to Joram, son of Ahab.

Elisha is known for performing many miracles. He divided the Jordan River so that he might pass from one side to the other (2 Kings 2:13). He caused a widow's empty cruse of oil to fill at his command (2 Kings 4:1–7). He blessed a barren Shunammite woman and she conceived (2 Kings 4: 14–17). He raised a child from the dead (2 Kings 4:35), and he cured the Aramean captain Naaman of leprosy (2 Kings 5).

Ezekiel

Little is known of Ezekiel's life. His father's name was Buzi and he was likely a member of the priestly family of Zadok. Among those Judeans forced into exile by the Babylonians in 586 B.C.E., he lived in a Jewish colony in Babylon called Tel Aviv. It was there that he had his vision of the Throne-Chariot of God and became a prophet.

Ezekiel began prophesying in the fifth year of Jehoiachin's exile, and his work as a prophet lasted at least twenty-two years. Ezekiel's vision of Israel is dark and disturbing. He sees the people of Israel as forever falling into sin and rebellion against God.

A master of prophetic theater, Ezekiel's prophecies are often accompanied by dramatic acts: He eats a scroll of lamentation (Ezekiel 2:9–3:3); draws Jerusalem on a clay tablet and lays siege to it (Ezekiel 4:1–8); bakes loaves of barley over a stove fueled by human manure to make plain the unclean foods the people will be forced to eat in exile (Ezekiel 4:12–13); and shaves his head and beard, using the hair to symbolize Israel—burning a third with fire, cutting a third with a sword, and scattering a third to the wind (Ezekiel 5).

Habakkuk

Little is known of Habakkuk's life, other than that he lived in Judah in the early 600s B.C.E. His short book of prophecy, comprising three chapters and fifty-six verses, contains what the later rabbis (*Makkot* 24a) took to be the heart of Judaism: "The just shall live by faith" (2:4). *Faith* here means "trust," trusting that the injustices decried by the prophet, especially the exploitation of the Jews at the hand of the Chaldeans, will come to an end through the saving power of God.

Haggai

Based on four prophetic experiences in the year 520 B.C.E., Haggai chides the people of Israel to redouble their efforts to rebuild the Temple in Jerusalem. He assures them that this new Temple, while modest in comparison to its predecessor, the Temple of King Solomon, will someday come to rival it in majesty. Despite his focus on the Temple, however, Haggai warns the people that deeds, not animal sacrifice, are the key to holiness. Rebuilding the Temple cannot guarantee holiness; only rebuilding your life on a foundation of justice and compassion can do that.

Hosea

Hosea tells us next to nothing about his personal life. The one detail that he does share—God commanding him to marry a prostitute to symbolize Israel's disloyalty to God, and his subsequent marriage to Gomer, who bears him three children—may be more metaphor than history. Hosea had a series of prophetic revelations during the reigns of the Judean kings Uzziah (769–733 B.C.E.), Jothan, Ahaz, and Hezekiah (758–698 B.C.E.), and the Israelite kings Jeroboam II and Menahem (784–737 B.C.E.). Hosea attacks the people for being disloyal to God and worshiping the Canaanite god Baal. He berates the kings of Israel for foreign entanglements, another sign of disloyalty to God; and warns all the people that rigorous adherence to cultic ritual is meaningless if one's treatment of other people is exploitative and immoral. The sages of the Talmud say that Hosea was a contemporary of fellow prophets Isaiah, Amos, and Micah, and that of the four Hosea is the greatest (*Pesach* 87a).

Isaiah

Isaiah tells us that he began to prophesy in 733 B.C.E., the year Uzziah, king of Judah, died. Scholars believe that Isaiah was a Levite working in the Temple and perhaps of noble birth, given his ready access to the inner circle of the Judean court. Isaiah has two sons and names them as part of his prophecy. The elder he calls *Shear-yashuv*, "a remnant shall return." This is a name of hope, promising King Ahaz and the Judean people that they will survive the coming attack by Syria and her Northern Kingdom ally (Israel). His second son he calls *Maher-shalal-hash-baz*, "the spoil speeds, the prey hastens," suggesting that the Northern Kingdom of Israel will disappear when the Assyrians defeat the Syrians and their allies. In addition to warning the kings of their political follies, Isaiah relentlessly challenges the people to live up to the moral standards set for them by God. Putting one's hope in politics is madness, Isaiah says. Hope is only in God and God is only concerned with righteousness. While in no way sparing the people the full impact of God's impending wrath, Isaiah does comfort them with a vision of a future when peace will reign: The lion shall lie down with the lamb, and swords will be beaten into plowshares.

Jeremiah

Beginning in 626 B.C.E., Jeremiah prophesied for over four decades, speaking to the people about the larger meaning of the fall of the Assyrian Empire, the rise of Babylonia, the Judean alliance with Egypt in response to Babylonian power, and the subsequent fall of Egypt and Judah to Babylon, resulting in the first exile of the Jews from their homeland (586 B.C.E.). Thought to be a traitor by both kings and commoners, Jeremiah urges the people to submit to Babylonian hegemony. When the Babylonians conquer Judah and exile her elite, Jeremiah is left behind to pacify the people. With the assassination of Gedaliah, the Babylonian-appointed governor of Judah, Jeremiah joins the rest of the Judean elite in a hasty departure to Egypt, fearing that they will be punished by Babylon for the death of Gedaliah. In Egypt, Jeremiah continues his work, attacking the Jews of Egypt for their idolatrous relationship to the Egyptian gods.

Joel

Nothing is known about Joel's life, and even the time of his prophecy is open to debate. Joel restricts himself to addressing the Kingdom of Judah alone, suggesting that he was himself a Judean, and may have lived after the fall of the Northern Kingdom of Israel. Some scholars note Joel's references to the Temple in Jerusalem as the sole place of worship, suggesting that he lived after the building of the second Temple (515 B.C.E.) but before the Persian conquest (348 B.C.E.). Others, noting that Joel makes no reference to a king of Judah, argue that he must have lived after the fall of Judah to the Persians. The essence of Joel's message is to warn the people of the coming Day of the Lord, a day of judgment marked by a plague of locusts. He calls upon the people to repent, to pray, fast, and mourn, and promises the repentant—both Jew and Gentile alike—that God will deliver them from disaster.

Jonah

The Book of Jonah is more a short story about the prophet than a collection of his prophecies. Jonah is commanded by God to warn the forty thousand inhabitants of Nineveh, a people hostile to the Israelites, that their evil actions will have dire consequences. Worried that the people of Nineveh will indeed repent and, in so doing, make the unrepentant Jews look bad, Jonah seeks to avoid God's command by fleeing from Jaffa to Tarshish. He reasons that the God of the Jews is restricted to the land of the Jews, and cannot exert power outside that land. The Jonah story, a tale about a prophet rather than the teachings of a prophet, makes this one point: There is only one God and that God is God of all creation. Jonah is tossed into the sea to save the ship from destruction and is carried off to Nineveh inside a great fish. Jonah preaches the word of God to the people of Nineveh and they do repent and earn God's forgiveness, thus proving the point that God is the God of all peoples.

Malachi

Malachi may be the name of a prophet or it may be a title, meaning as it does "My messenger." We know nothing about Malachi as a person, and there is no certainty about when his prophecies were spoken. From the contents of the book, modern scholars date Malachi sometime after the rebuilding of the Temple and before the reforms instituted by Ezra and Nehemiah. Going even further than Jonah in spreading the message of God's universalism, God speaks through Malachi, saying, "From where the sun rises to where it sets, My Name is honored among the nations" (1:11). In addition to his emphasis on God's universalism, Malachi is the first person to link the return of the prophet Elijah with the redemption of the world.

Micah

Prophesying in the latter half of the eighth century B.C.E. during the reigns of Judah's kings Jotham, Ahaz, and Hezekiah (c. 758–698 B.C.E.), Micah came from the Judean town of Moreshet-Gat. Despite his ties to Judah, however, Micah addresses his prophecies to both the Northern Kingdom of Israel and the Southern Kingdom of Judah. Micah is the first of the prophets to foretell the destruction of Jerusalem and to link that destruction to the idolatry and injustices of the city's inhabitants. Micah challenges both political and economic elites, warning the rulers of the doom their policies are engendering, and denouncing dishonest business practices. His most famous utterance is among Judaism's most universal teachings: that God's only demand of humanity is to "do justly, love mercy, and walk humbly with your God" (6:8).

Obadiah

Obadiah's prophecies constitute the shortest book of the Bible: a single chapter with twenty-one verses. Nothing is known about the prophet himself. He tells us neither his father's name nor the city of his birth. The best scholars can do is place him sometime after the fall of Judah to the Babylonians in 586 B.C.E. This date rests on the polemical nature of his prophecy aimed at the Edomites. The Edomites sided with Babylonia and against Judah, and collaborated with the former, attacking refugees and occupying the Negev. Obadiah speaks of God's wrath against the Edomites, promising to crush them and turn their possessions over to the House of Jacob.

Samuel

Samuel plays a crucial role in the history of Israel. The last of the judges who rule Israel prior to its becoming a monarchy, Samuel is also a prophet. The son of Elkanah and Hannah, Samuel is a gift to his mother from God. Praying at the Sanctuary in Shiloh before the priest Eli, Hannah begs God for a son and promises to turn the boy over to the priest to be raised as a servant of God. God grants her wish, and, after Samuel is weaned, Hannah gives him to Eli. God visits Samuel with a prophecy, showing him the future destruction of Shiloh and the House of Eli. When this comes to pass, Samuel is recognized as a prophet and appointed a judge over Israel. In time, Samuel's two sons, Joel and Abiyah, are also named judges but they are unjust, and the people demand that Samuel appoint a king over Israel and put an end to the system of judges. Samuel resists, but God commands him to anoint Saul as king, which he does after warning the people of the dangers of a monarchy. Saul fails to live up to the demands of God, and Samuel prophesies that his reign is at an end, secretly anointing David as king. On the eve of Saul's battle with the Philistines on Mount Gilboa, the witch of En-dor raises Samuel from the dead for a final prophecy in which he foretells the death of Saul and Saul's sons.

Zechariah

A contemporary of the prophet Haggai, Zechariah prophesied for only two years, 522 to 520 B.C.E. At the heart of Zechariah's message is the assurance to the returning Israelites that the rebuilding of the Temple after the Babylonian exile is the precursor to the messianic age. Along with Haggai, Zechariah fights to overcome the depression that has settled on the Jews upon their return to Judah. The country is in ruins, the people are demoralized, and the Temple is a pale reflection of its former glory. Rather than allow the people to fall into despair, seeing their lives only in the shadow of God's wrath, Zechariah urges them to regain their confidence and have faith in the coming apocalyptic transformation of their fate, so they once again become the beloved of God.

Zephaniah

Claiming to be a descendant of King Hezekiah and therefore a distant relative of King Josiah against whom he prophesied (639–609 B.C.E.), Zephaniah is called the "Prophet of the Day of the Lord," warning the rulers of Judah that God will raise a global army of the righteous against them, leaving only a remnant of Judah to inherit God's grace and be returned to their former glory. In addition to attacking the rulers, Zephaniah also attacks the common people for idol worship. Ultimately, however, his is a prophecy of hope, promising that if the people of Judah repent, they will become the model of justice and peace for the entire world.

The Mission
of the Prophets

1 What is it to be seduced by God? The prophet desires love and justice for and from humanity, and is thus seduced by God's promise of both. What he doesn't realize is that the prophet himself will find none of it.

2 What is it to be overpowered by God? The prophet had doubts, but God's assurance of ultimate victory removed those doubts. No matter how much resistance one has to love, in the end love will win out.

3 The prophet's mission is to hold a mirror up to your foolish and destructive behaviors—not a job that endears one to those who are mirrored. Where might you be laughing at the very people who are pointing out the errors in your life?

4 The prophet is often reluctant to speak, knowing that the message will bring the messenger much pain. But in the end the prophet has no choice, and is compelled to speak by a blazing sense of God's presence and urgency. This is what it is to be a prophet: to risk a life of derision and torment because your love of God and humanity is so great that you cannot but do otherwise.

The prophet Jeremiah said:

"You seduced me, God, and I was seduced.[1]
You overpowered me and You won.[2]
I have become a constant laughingstock.[3]
Everyone jeers at me
for every time I speak I shout out the lawlessness
and evil of my neighbors.
This is Your word and it causes me unending disgrace
and contempt.

I tried to suppress Your Word.
I said to myself: I will not mention God
or speak God's Name.
But Your word burned in my heart like a raging fire
setting my very bones ablaze.
I could not keep silent. I was helpless."[4]

—JEREMIAH 20:7–9

1 Here is the mission of the prophet: to be the emissary of God and godliness.

2 The prophet is one who hears God's call and responds: *Hineini,* Here I am. This is the response of every truly spiritual person: "Here I am at this very moment ready to meet the challenges of the moment that I might bring forth justice and compassion."

3 The prophet is sent not to those who cannot hear, but to those who choose not to hear; not to those who cannot see, but to those who choose not to see. Where do you stuff your ears against the cries of injustice? Where do you close your eyes to the plight of others?

4 It is the task of the prophet to unstuff your ears and uncover your eyes so that you will hear, see, and respond to the needs of the world with justice and mercy. But there is more; for your response to others also softens your own heart that you might turn from the deadening errors of your life, heal the suffering that they have caused, and live no longer plagued by fear and hesitation.

The One Who Is says:

"Whom shall I send? Who will go for us?"[1]
And I said, "Here am I; send me."[2]
And God said, "Go, say to that people:
'You hear, but you do not understand;
you see, but you do not grasp.'[3]
Their hearts grow fat,
they stuff their ears and cover their eyes,
lest they hear and see and soften their hearts so they
might repent and heal."[4]

—ISAIAH 6:8–10

1 Ahab was king over Israel from 871 to 852 B.C.E. His wife, Jezebel, sought to make Baal worship the state religion, supporting 450 priests of Baal and 400 priestesses of his consort Astarte, and promoting the persecution of the prophets of YHVH.

2 Troubling you is the prophet's task. It is the prophet's job to disturb your complacency; challenging you to look at your life honestly, and see whom you are worshiping: God or Baal.

3 Trouble comes not from the prophet, but from the choices you make. The prophet simply shines the clear light of truth on your life and allows you to see your choices and the consequences they carry.

4 What are the commandments at the heart of the prophetic vision? Do justly, love mercy, and walk humbly with your God (Micah 6:8).

5 *Baal* (singular); *baalim* (plural) means "lord" and refers both to the chief Canaanite fertility god and to all false gods. A god is false when it is the work of your imagination, devoted to excusing selfishness and blinding you to your freedom to choose.

King Ahab said to the prophet Elijah:[1]

"Is that you, you troubler of Israel?"[2]

Elijah said, "It's not me who troubles Israel,
but you and your regime,[3]
for you have abandoned the commandments[4] of the
One Who Is
and have gone after the baalim."[5]
—1 KINGS 18:17–18

1 Hopping between two opinions, vacillating between what is true and what is false, is one way to avoid the hard choice of following the One Who Is. In the Zen tradition there is a saying: "When hungry eat; when tired sleep; but above all don't wobble." Jesus said something similar when he said, "Let what you say be simply 'Yes' or 'No'; anything more than this comes from evil" (Matthew 5:37). Elijah is challenging you to simplify the chatter in your mind and see that the choice before you is simple: truth or falsehood, selflessness or selfishness, the One Who Is or the one who isn't.

2 There are two types of spiritual silence. There is the silence of awakening: "Be still and know that I am God" (Psalm 46:10), and there is the silence of confusion. The first is simple: There is nothing to say, nothing to add to the completeness that is God. The second is complicated: There is nothing to say that will save you from having to admit that you are choosing wrongly. This silence is a strategy of self-delusion. The prophet's task is to make you aware of where you are fooling yourself so that you might choose to do otherwise.

The prophet Elijah says:

> "How long will you keep hopping between
> two opinions?[1]
> If the One Who Is is God, follow God;
> but if Baal is God, follow him!"
>
> The people answered him not a word.[2]

—1 KINGS 18:21

1 Where do you hide to avoid dealing with the fact of your indecision, your wobbling? God calls you out of hiding; God calls you to wake up. And one of the ways God does this is through the prophets themselves.

2 Tornadoes, earthquakes, raging fires—these are things that demand your attention. You do not choose to take note of them; you cannot help yourself. But God is otherwise. God is subtle; easily ignored and overlooked. The silence that is God is the awareness of God in, with, and as you.

3 The prophets hear this silence and feel themselves addressed, commanded. The silence of God is empty of content but full of intent. In that silence you grow silent. In that silence you let go of all you think you know about who you are and what you are to do. And in that place of not-knowing, you experience yourself being asked: Why are you here? The answer? To do justly, to love mercy, and to walk humbly. And, in the case of the prophets, to call others to do the same.

The One Who Is says:

"Come out and stand before the One Who Is."[1]

Suddenly the One Who Is passed by.
A huge and powerful tornado swept by Elijah,
splitting mountains and shattering rocks,
but the One Who Is was not in the tornado.
The tornado passed, followed by a violent quaking of
the earth,
but the One Who Is was not in the earthquake.
The earth grew still and a roaring fire
consumed the earth;
but the One Who Is was not in the blaze.
Then the fire burned out, replaced by a fragile silence.[2]

Elijah heard it, and wrapped his cloak about his face
and stood at the mouth of the cave.
Then a voice addressed him:
"Why are you here, Elijah?"[3]

—1 Kings 19:11–13

[**1**] Much of what you consume is poisoning you. The amount of calories you eat; the quantities of violence you absorb; the weight of your possessions; the overwhelming amount of data that inundates you daily—all of this and more is burying you alive. You are drowning in a sea of choice that gives you no guidelines for choosing wisely. You no longer know how to tell the difference between truth and well-packaged lies.

[**2**] The prophet knows how to transform what you consume. He adds a bit of flour, the staff of life; the truth of justice, kindness, and humility; and you can eat and be satisfied.

[**3**] The prophets' task is to help you eat in a way that feeds both self and other. There are two aspects of this mission. The first is to demonstrate the falsity of zero-sum thinking: The pie is not fixed; there is enough for all. The second is to invite you to partake of the banquet that is God's bounty in a way that reveals that you are filled only when others are sated as well. If even one stomach goes hungry, yours too should growl at the injustice. This story most likely provides the impetus for the tale of Jesus feeding the masses with five loaves of bread and two fish (Matthew 14:17ff).

The disciples of Elisha said:

"Man of God, there is death in the pot!"[1]
Elisha said, "Fetch some flour."
He threw a handful into the pot and the poison
disappeared.[2]
"Now, serve it to the people and let them eat."

A man came … and brought Elisha twenty loaves of
barley bread,
and some fresh grain in his sack.
Elisha said, "Give it to the people and let them eat."
His attendant replied, "How can I set so little before a
hundred men?"
But Elisha said, "Give it to the people and let them eat.
For thus said the One Who Is: 'They shall eat and have
some left over.'"
So he set it before them; and when they had eaten,
they had some left over,
as the One Who Is had said.[3]

—2 KINGS 4:40–44

1 A shofar is a ram's horn. The ancient Hebrew equivalent to a modern early warning siren, the shofar is blown to warn people of impending disaster. The blowing of the shofar is also a central part of the High Holy Day rituals. In this case, the shofar warns you of the disaster you are causing in your own life by failing to live justly, kindly, and humbly.

2 God is the sole reality, thus evil must come from God. You may prefer to think of God as only good, only just, only kind, and so on. But the truth is that God is everything: light and dark, good and evil, blessing and curse. You see this throughout the prophets: God is both the cause of calamity and the source of salvation. How are you to understand this?

Think in terms of electricity running through an outlet in your home. If you plug a lamp into the socket, you receive light. If you stick your finger in the socket, you get electrocuted. The nature of electricity hasn't changed; how you engage it has. It is the same with God. Engage God wisely and goodness results; engage God foolishly and disaster occurs. What is engaging God wisely? Living justly, compassionately, and humbly. What is engaging God foolishly? Living unjustly, cruelly, and exploiting all you meet.

3 Here is another aspect of the prophetic task: to sound a warning so you look to your actions to see if you are not about to stick your finger in the socket and die.

The One Who Is says:

Can two walk together without meeting?
Does a lion roar in the forest if it has no prey?
Does a beast let out a cry from its den if it has not
trapped its meal?
Does a bird suddenly fall to the ground unless snared?
Does a trap spring up from the ground without having
caught something?
When a shofar sounds in a town,
do the people not worry?[1]
Can misfortune befall a place if the One Who Is
has not caused it?[2]
Indeed, the One Who Is does nothing
without first revealing it to the divine servants the
prophets.[3]

—AMOS 3:1–7

1 A prophet acts as a siren whose task is to warn you when you are about to set out on the path of self-destruction. The prophet reminds you of the principles of holy living: justice, kindness, humility, awareness, and the like. It is up to you to heed the warning and change your behavior.

2 If God always warns you before you make a mistake, and if the prophet is compelled to make sure you are given that warning, why is it so difficult to stay on the true path? The answer is that most of the time God's warning is subtle. The books of the prophets make it seem that at every critical juncture some bearded wild man will leap out from the shadows and warn you of the consequences of the action you are about to take. But it isn't that obvious. The prophetic warning comes in quiet ways—a tightening in your belly; a furtive glance to see if you are being seen; a sudden upswing in your heart rate; a feeling of guilt, anxiety, and lowered self-esteem. These do not always portend disaster, but they are often the voice of the prophet calling you to pay attention not only to what you are about to do, but also to the inevitable consequences that will be set in motion if you do it.

The One Who Is says:

I have appointed you as a siren over the
House of Israel.
Whenever you hear a message from My mouth,
you must transmit My warning to them.[1]
If I say to the wicked, "You shall die,"
and you have not warned them of the consequences
of their actions,
not only shall they perish for their sins,
but I will demand a reckoning for their blood from you.
But if you have warned the wicked to turn back from
their ways,
and they have not turned from them, they shall die for
their own sins,
but you will have saved your life.[2]

—EZEKIEL 33:7–9

From Ignorance...
...to Truth

1 There is no bargaining with God. Reality is reality. Actions have consequences. You reap what you sow. But with idols things are different.
Idolatry is all about bargaining: "I will do this for you, if you do this
for me." Whenever you are bargaining for life to be other than it is
without your having to act differently than you are, you are worshiping
idols.

2 When you cry out to God, do so with a broken heart. A broken
heart, a heart no longer seduced by lies and false hope, sees clearly
the choice before you: ignorance or truth, injustice or justice, despair or
joy. The starkness of the choice revives your power to choose. And perhaps this time you will choose God.

3 You are faithless to God when you are faithful to things. You are
faithless to God when you imagine that your happiness lies outside of
you in the externals of the world. You are faithless to God when you
place your fate in the hands of others, rather than in the hands of the
One Who Is your truest self.

The One Who Is says:

Thus will I punish you for your bargaining....[1]
I would have saved you,
but even as you lay crying on your bed, your heart
didn't cry out to Me.[2]
You gather together in orgies of profit,
and you are faithless to Me.[3]

—HOSEA 7:12–15

1 If you are not sincere in your calling out to God, there can be no response. All you will hear is a hollow echo of your shallow cry. The hallmark of sincere crying out to God is a feeling of absolute powerlessness. You have tried everything, and everything has failed. Only God can save you, but you have so much invested in lies that you cannot muster the power to turn. It is then that God saves you, and gives you the courage to turn even when you are certain you cannot turn. This is the salvation of God: the courage to turn and do differently in the present than you have done in the past.

2 False gods are everywhere. They dwell where you dwell, both physically and psychologically. Look around your life: Where have you invested things with power and meaning? Where have you placed your Hope? In money? Power? Clothes? Image? Sex? A spouse or partner? There is only one place to invest yourself: in just, compassionate, and humble action.

The One Who Is says:

You are ashamed, but there is no sincerity in it ...[1]
Like thieves caught in the act, you feign contrition.
It is not the act you regret, but getting caught!

You say to blocks of wood, "You are my father,"
and to slabs of stone, "You gave birth to me."
While to Me you turn your back and do not
show your face.
Yet, in your hour of need, you will cry out to Me,
"Arise and save us!"

Where are your gods then?
Let them rise up and save you.
You certainly do not lack for gods,
they have become as numerous as your desires![2]

—JEREMIAH 2:26–28

1 The way of fools is always the way of imitation. Imitating the lives of others means never living out your own uniqueness and potentiality. It is turning your back on the gift of life. Idols demand imitation; God demands authenticity.

2 Your horoscope promises you a destiny without demanding a deed. The stars fix your character; all you need do is accept it. God offers no fixed destiny, only the power of choice. "I have set before you life and death, blessing and curse; therefore choose ..." (Deuteronomy 30:19).

3 What is the delusion of idolatry? That freedom is a gift not a choice. No one can set you free. You must choose to be free each moment of your life. An idol promises you freedom; God promises you only choice. The first choice is between God and the idol itself. If you choose the latter, it is the last choice you may ever make.

4 Why do you fear idols? Because you know that if you abandon them, you will have to choose for yourself how to live, and this you don't want to do. You would rather drown in misery, pretending not to have a choice, then take responsibility for your suffering and choose to live differently. The fear of the idol is really fear of responsibility.

The One Who Is says:

Do not imitate the way of fools.[1]
Do not distract yourself with zodiacs and signs,
no matter how many are captivated by them.[2]

You are deluded by the wisdom of fools.[3]
Your faith is in the work of your own hands.
You cut down trees in the forest with an ax,
adorn them with silver and gold,
fasten them with nails and hammer so as to keep
them from tottering.
These are your gods! They are like scarecrows for
frightening birds.
They do not speak. They cannot walk.
They can do no harm and intend you no good; and yet
you are afraid of them.[4]

—JEREMIAH 10:1–5

1 True satisfaction comes from living each moment with authenticity. Doing so means knowing and accepting yourself—the good and the bad, the wise and the foolish parts of yourself—and then choosing to nurture the former even as you shepherd the latter. When you live with authenticity, you live without fear. You have nothing to hide because even your mistakes are out in the open. You are no longer vulnerable to the pretense of perfection, and you can laugh at your foibles even as you are humbled by them. Satisfaction comes not from being perfect, but from being true.

2 Instead of living with authenticity, you choose to follow the way of fools, the way of imitation. You model your life on externals and allow them to dictate your speech, your dress, your work, and your honor. No matter how successful an imitator you are, there is no satisfaction in imitation. Your hunger for authenticity grows alongside your imitation success. Why do you do this? Because you think it will win the admiration of others, but they know you are a fake, for they too are fakes, and will use your imitation as the butt of jokes to distract them from the poverty of their own lives.

The One Who Is says:

You eat without satisfaction.[1]
Your stomach is full and yet groans with hunger.
You conceive without giving birth,
and those who do, see their young murdered in
infancy.
You sow without harvest.
You press olives but there is no oil.
Your crush grapes but they yield no juice.

Yet you continue to follow the ways of fools
and make of yourselves objects of derision
and the butt of jokes.[2]

—MICAH 6:14–16

1 At the heart of all spiritual work is the act of turning. Turning is a radical act of redirection that aligns you with God and godliness at the very instant you turn. There is nothing to believe, no creed to follow, no church to join. There is only your decision to turn and the turning itself.

You may hide from the power of turning by imagining there is more to it than there is. Say, for example, you see yourself as a liar. You invest heavily in this definition and imagine that you must undo some deep-seated illness before you can free yourself of being a liar. But God says differently. Don't worry about being a liar; simply choose to tell the truth. There is no permanent "you"; there is only the "you" that emerges from each decision and deed.

The One Who Is says:

Do not be like your forebears!
When the earlier prophets called to them, saying,
"Thus said the One Who Is:
'Come, turn back from your evil ways and
your evil deeds,'"
they did not obey or give heed to Me.[1]

—ZECHARIAH 1:4

1 What is it you need to know and comprehend? That God is your source and your substance. The Book of Genesis tells you that you are made in the image and likeness of God (Genesis 1:27). Your relation to God is like that of a wave to the ocean, a ray of sunlight to the sun. There is an intimacy in this relationship that surpasses understanding. You are the One Who Is manifest in you as you.

2 Why do you exist? There is only one answer: to know you are God manifest in your unique time and place. You are the way God knows Itself. You are the way God takes out the trash, walks the dog, cooks breakfast, and goes to the toilet. You are the way God does justly, kindly, and compassionately. Do not imagine you are high or low, sinner or saint, means or end. You are the One Itself.

The One Who Is says:

> An ox knows its owner,
> an ass its master's feeding trough;
> but you do not know,
> you do not comprehend....[1]

—ISAIAH 1:3

> Does an ax boast,
> "I am greater than the lumberjack"?
> Does a saw swell up with pride, saying,
> "I am greater than the carpenter"?
> Does a rod raise the builder?
> Does a staff lift the holder?[2]

—ISAIAH 10:15

1 Fear is the hallmark of the foolish. Where you are afraid, there you are foolish. Most people equate fear with the unknown, but we cannot fear what we do not know. Fear is fear of the known projected on the unknown. We take what we already fear in the past and imagine it happening in some form in the future. Thus the real problem with foolishness is that it traps you in time.

And this is what you have forgotten: God is the Present. God is reality manifest in this moment. To be present to God is to be free from past and future. To be free from past and future is to be free from fear. To be free from fear is to live with the joy that arises from trusting the moment to be whatever it needs to be, and trusting yourself to engage it fully.

The One Who Is says:

> The foolish are frightened by the dark
> and by morning they have disappeared.
> This is the fate of those who have forgotten.[1]
>
> —ISAIAH 17:14

1 Wisdom is not for the young. To understand life you must have experienced living. Wisdom is not for the masters of rote learning. They only know the past, and are desperate to stuff the present into it. Wisdom is not for the foolish. They simply repeat what they have heard without ever asking whether or not it is true. Wisdom is not for the easily distracted. They mistake content for knowledge, and collect ideas as another might collect stamps.

Wisdom is for those who have lived long enough to know they do not know. Wisdom is for those who realize that truth is not found in a book. Wisdom is for those who question the past, and enter fully into the present without shield or shelter. Wisdom is for those who challenge authority, who do not mistake pious opinion for timeless truth. Wisdom is for those whose minds are stable, who have learned to settle and see what is without being distracted by what might be next.

The One Who Is says:

> To whom should I offer wisdom?
> To whom should I explain the message?
> To infants newly weaned, barely taken from their
> mother's breast?
> To those whose learning is but rote muttering?
> To those who mumble nonsense packaged as truth?
> To those whose minds wobble from this to that, and
> know no stability?[1]
>
> —ISAIAH 28:9–10

1 God desires your heart. Your mind can rationalize anything, but your heart knows what is true and what is false. Your heart rejoices at the former and troubles itself over the latter.

2 You worship gods of your own invention. Religion is imitative; God is not. Religion serves the past; God serves the present. Religion elevates the believer; God elevates only truth.

3 The consequence of living by imitation is lifelessness. The consequence of lifeless living is alienation from God. Not that God is ever other than you, but you feel other than God. You then worship idols to fill the void you imagine. In so doing, you further blind yourself to truth, and seek to blind others as well.

The One Who Is says:

Because you approach Me with mouth and lips,
and not your heart;[1]
because your worship is imitative,[2]
learned by rote and mumbled lifelessly,
I will confound you further.[3]

Wisdom and marvels will I offer you,
but you will not understand.
Your sages will seem foolish,
and your pious will seem imprudent.
—ISAIAH 29:13–14

1   Triumph is right living. Right living is rooted in quiet stillness. You spend so much energy running around from thing to thing, experience to experience, distraction to distraction in hopes of maintaining the illusion that you are in control. Your motto is Hunter Thompson's "Faster and faster until the thrill of speed overcomes the fear of death." There is no salvation in this fearful racing around. Be still and know that the One Who Is is God (Psalm 46:10).

2   You cannot outrun reality. The things you fear, the things from which you flee, are always waiting for you at the finish line. There is no escape from yourself, and it is yourself you fear most of all. Not the spacious self that knows itself to be one with God, but the narrow self that feeds on the illusion of power and control. Do not seek to escape the narrow self. Simply stop feeding it with distractions; sit quietly and allow it to subside of its own accord.

The One Who Is says:

Triumph comes through stillness and quiet;
Victory comes through calm and confidence.[1]
But you do not listen.
Instead you declare,
"I shall mount a swift horse and outrun my enemies."
Good—I made the horses of your enemies
swifter still....[2]
—ISAIAH 30:15–17

1 There is no security, no surety. There is only the unfolding of life, moment to moment. God is asking you live without certainty; knowing only the way (justice, kindness, and compassion) and giving no thought to the destination.

2 Where do you hide from uncertainty? In holy books and ancient teachings? In pious pomp? In sacred groves? Even contemplation can be a hideout if you use it to avoid the moment as it is and live in the fantasy of your own mind.

3 Your escape from unknowing is escape into the narrow self and the illusion of control. Are you in control of your life? You may think so; but the prophets think otherwise.

4 There is no one to save you. And you cannot save yourself. The self that got you into the mess of your life cannot get you out. The narrow self of certainty is the source of the problem, not the solution. All you can do is the one thing you fear doing most: Face the truth and let the narrow self surrender under the weight of its own delusion.

The One Who Is says:

> Pay attention, you pampered fool.
> Your security is a lie....[1]
>
> You take refuge in your own ignorance.[2]
> Your skill and your science feed your delusion:
> you imagine you reign supreme....[3]
>
> You are helpless despite your skill.
> Call your sages for help: the conjurers and stargazers
> whose horoscopes are your monthly guides.
> They are as straw to the flame;
> even as they burn, they leave no coal to
> keep you warm....
> There is no one to save you.[4]
>
> —ISAIAH 47:8–14

From Ignorance…
…to Truth

[1] You are what you do. You are not what you did or what you intend
to do. You are what you do here and now. You may have a long
résumé documenting extraordinary acts of kindness, but if in this
moment you act cruelly, you are, for the moment, cruel. You may have
a rap sheet a mile long, but if you act justly and mercifully in this
moment you are, for the moment, a blessing. There is nothing other
than this moment, and your act of engaging this moment. Your past
does not define you. Only your decision as to how to engage the present can do that. And even then, it does it only for the moment.

The One Who Is says,

> When the righteous do evil,
> their righteousness cannot save them.
> When the wicked turn to the good,
> their sins will not cause them to stumble.
>
> When I say, "The righteous shall surely live,"
> this does not mean they can rely on their righteousness
> to save them if they choose evil.
> So, too, when I say, "The wicked shall surely die,"
> this does not mean they cannot turn and live.[1]

—EZEKIEL 33:12–19

1 | Where are you trusting in mute idols? Look around you. Can you see where the work of your hands has somehow gotten the upper hand in your life? Can you see where your possessions possess you? What do you trust these things to do for you? Until you recognize the idols before which you worship, you will never be able to turn to the One Who Is and be free.

2 | Where is the abode of God? The abode of God is reality itself. You dwell in God as God right now. This is the good news of the prophets. All you have to do is be silent in the moment; experience what is rather than what your chattering mind wishes there to be. When you are silent, you silence delusion and falsehood, and realize the simple truth of God in, with, and as all things. Seeing the truth allows you to live truthfully. And that is what God requires of you.

The One Who Is says:

Of what value is the carved image even to the carver?
Molten statues teach you nothing,
so why do you trust in idols?[1]

Only a fool says to wood, "Wake up!"
or to lifeless stone, "Arise!"
Can a coating of gold and silver disguise the fact
that there is no breath within it?

But I reside in My holy abode—
Be silent before Me all the earth![2]

—HABAKKUK 2:18–20

1 What is the place to which God returns? It is not a place in time or space. It is a place in heart and mind. God hides from you in plain sight, and you choose not to see. You imagine that to find God you must change yourself, but this is simply the ego's way of avoiding seeing God in, with, and as all things. As long as you have to be other than you are, the ego can bemoan that it is what it is. How do you seek God's Face? By accepting what is, and not by promising to change it. You must admit your imperfection fully. In the midst of your imperfection, you will find the One who embraces imperfection. Your idols promise you perfection. God promises you reality.

2 Your ego loves the idea of sacrifice, saying: "I must sacrifice the smaller self to the greater self, and then I will find peace." This is a trap. There is no sacrifice of ego by ego. The very effort bolsters the power of the smaller self. God doesn't want you to sacrifice the small self; God wants you to realize your greater self and in this way free the small self from selfishness.

The One Who Is says:

I am leaving you;
I am returning to My place until you
acknowledge your error
and seek My Face; in your distress you will seek Me ...[1]

... For I desire kindness, not sacrifice;
knowledge of God, rather than burnt offerings.[2]

—HOSEA 5:15; 6:6

1 God is no stranger to you. God is your mother, your father. God has recognized you as a divine child and yet you continue to worship ideas and idols that blind you to the intimacy of God's love. Why? Because God's love is unconditional, and you prefer the conditional. You live in a conditioned world, a world of bargains, a world of winning and losing. You want to win, and imagine that you have to do something to make this happen, but there is nothing you need to do. Nothing but know the truth and live it.

2 God pampers you, providing for all your needs, but you insist that you must do for yourself, and then, realizing that you cannot succeed, you plead with false gods for that which you already have but will not accept.

3 God offers you everything you desire, but the god you choose to worship, the god of your imagination or the imagination of others, feeds you nothing. Rather than turn from the false to the true, you invent theologies that make God your enemy, sealing your mouth so that the food you desire is unattainable by you. You do this, not God. The food is right there; you just refuse to eat it.

The One Who Is says:

I fell in love with you when you were still a child;
and I have called you My child ever since Egypt;[1]
but to no avail; you went your own way,
sacrificing to false gods and burning incense
to carved blocks.

I have pampered you,
cradling you in My arms;
but you have ignored My healing care.[2]

I drew you to Me in the way of human love,
I offered you food,
but you insisted upon seeing Me as one who lays a
yoke upon you,
wiring shut your jaws.[3]

—HOSEA 11:1–4

1 God is beyond talk. A god who can be reduced to words is not the true God. The prophets understand God as the One Who Is, the absolute reality in which your relative reality dwells. When you think of God in terms of your relative experience, you reduce God to an idol of your tribe, your religion, your nationality, your desires. God is beyond all of this.

2 How do you return to God? By engaging each moment with justice and compassion. To do this requires entering into the present moment without preconceptions. If you encounter the present with precon- ceptions (and all conceptions are in fact *pre*) you are not encountering the present at all, but rather your projection from the past onto the pre- sent. The present moment becomes an echo of the past. Idols speak in echoes, reflecting your own desires back to you as if they came from elsewhere. God is no echo. God speaks to you in the immediacy of the moment.

3 Trusting in God means living without a net. It means living with a radical sense of not-knowing. It is encountering the present without distractions of past and future. It is the scariest thing you can ever do.

The One Who Is says:

Invoke Me, the One Who Is, as All in all.[1]
Return to Me![2]
Practice compassion and justice,
and trust in Me always.[3]

—HOSEA 12:7

1　Do not imagine that you secure your own survival. Life is a gift, and living is being gifted moment to moment. You are not in control. You do not grow your hair, beat your heart, think your thoughts, or feel your feelings. All this happens but you are not the one who makes them happen. It is the way of the ego to imagine itself as god, to take credit for everything you have achieved, and to blame your failures on others. The challenge is to call out to God even in the midst of plenty, and in this way awaken to the truth that everything comes from God.

2　God desires the heart, and to get at it God sometimes rips it out of your frozen chest. At least this is how it seems. You can become so complacent, so sure of your own success and happiness, that you imagine you have no need for God. It is then that you need God the most. Your success becomes your idol; you worship it as proof of your own power and autonomy. But, in fact, you have little power and only vague autonomy. You do not control the moment, but only your response to the moment. Even the consequences of your response are outside your control. Do right because it is right. That is all you can know.

3　When you turn your back on God, you turn your attention to ego. You worship yourself, and this is the beginning of your destruction.

The One Who Is says:

I looked after you in the wilderness,
in the parched desert.
When you grazed, you became full;
when you were full, you grew haughty;
you forgot Me.[1]

So now I will become like a hungry lion among you;
like a famished leopard I will stalk you.
Like a bear robbed of her young,
I will maul you
and rip open the hardened shell of your heart;
I will devour you like a starving lion;
the beasts of the field shall split you open.[2]

You have destroyed yourselves,
turning your backs on Me, your only help.[3]

—HOSEA 13:5–9

1 This is the heart of the prophetic consciousness: All you have to do is return to your true nature. You need not fix what is broken, but turn in your brokenness and find a greater wholeness that embraces it. You do not have to be worthy of turning; you only have to turn.

2 God's love cannot be earned. It is a given. The only thing you need do is receive what is given. Receiving is not as easy as it sounds. Receiving God's love means accepting yourself as you are, honoring your imperfections, even as you do not allow them to dictate your actions. The prophet is saying: Do not prepare to turn, just turn; the change will take care of itself.

3 You must begin with yourself; you must turn. But you do not turn for yourself alone. Your turning and the changes it affects make you a mentor to others who can sit in the cool shade of your turning and turn themselves.

4 God's path is straight. It is saying what you mean and doing what you say. It is, as the Buddhists say, "not wobbling." There are no stumbling blocks on the way. The foolish stumble not because the way is hard, but because they wobble with indecision.

The One Who Is says:

Return to Me ...[1]
I will heal your suffering.
My love need not be earned,[2]
and My anger has turned away from you.
I will be to you like refreshing dew;
you shall blossom like the lily ...
your beauty shall be like the olive tree's,
your perfume like cedar.
All who sit in your shade shall be revived....[3]
I will turn toward you and look upon you.
I am an evergreen cypress,
providing you with all you need.
Are you wise enough to understand these things?
Can you grasp and know the truth?
The way of God is smooth;
the wise walk effortlessly,
the foolish stumble needlessly.[4]

—HOSEA 14:5–10

1 | The way of God is the way of being; the way of the baalim is the way of having. The way of being sees all beings as manifestations of God, and all encounters as holy meetings. The way of having regards all beings as means to an end, the end being your sense of power and control. Since you are never really in control, the life you live is fearful and bitter. You are a victim of your own delusion.

2 | Do not place ultimate trust in your own abilities. Everything you are and have is conditioned and conditional. Nothing is forever, except the One Who Is. Refuge, peace, harmony—all are found not in having but in being; not in playing god but in realizing that God is playing you.

3 | The way of God is not hidden or hard to know. It is simply living kindly, justly, and fairly. When others say to you that the way is difficult to master, they are deluded. When you say to yourself the way is hard to walk, you are excusing your own indecision.

The One Who Is says:

Because you forsake My teaching;
Because you do not heed My voice;
but choose rather to follow the passions of
your own hearts
and the ways of the baalim,[1]
you will feed on wormwood and drink
brackish water....

Let not the wise take refuge in their wisdom,
nor the strong in their strength,
nor the rich in their riches.
Seek refuge only in devotion to Me.[2]
For I, the One Who Is, act with kindness, justice,
and fairness in the world.
In these alone do I delight.[3]

—JEREMIAH 9:12–23

1 The real challenge of the prophets is in the simplicity of their demand: Turn. Don't worry about being worthy or acceptable to God. God will embrace you if you but turn around to be embraced. To turn requires no prerequisite. All there is is the decision to turn and the act of turning. These are one in the same. And so is the embrace of God that accompanies your turning. This is the unity and immediacy of decision and deed, and the overwhelming love from and for God that both release.

2 You may say to yourself: "I am too far gone to turn. I have done such horrible things; I am beyond the pale of God's love." This is simply your small self maintaining its hold over you. This is the voice of Baal distracting you from turning to God. It is the delusion that robs you of the truth and the love that comes with it. It is not that you must stop being a self-indulgent fool before you turn to God; it is that in turning to God as the self-indulgent fool, the fool becomes wise. Change nothing. Just turn.

The One Who Is says:

> If you turn back, I will take you back,[1]
> and you shall stand before Me.
> Even if you are a self-indulgent fool,
> if you turn toward honor, you shall be
> My mouthpiece....[2]
> I will rescue you from the hands of wickedness,
> and free you from the grip of violence.
>
> —JEREMIAH 15:19–21

1 What do you trust when you trust in transient things? You trust that they will somehow be immortal. You trust that the time-bound can lead to the timeless. It cannot.

2 Trusting in God means trusting in no-thing at all. Trusting in God means not mistaking the wave for the ocean, and yet not imagining it is "other" than the ocean either. Trusting in God means knowing that the parts partake of the whole, and the whole is timeless even as it encompasses time. Trusting in God means not mistaking the "you" you see in the mirror for the true "you," and yet not imagining that it is other than that you.

3 God does not free you from your folly, but allows you to taste the consequences of your choices until you are ready to choose differently. This is not punishment, but love.

The One Who Is says:

If you place your trust in the transient,
if you take refuge in flesh and blood rather than in Me,
you are doomed.[1]
You will become like scrub in the desert,
having no joy,
living only in scorched and barren wilderness.

Blessed are you who trust in Me, and in Me alone.[2]
You are like trees rooted near water.
Your leaves are evergreen and yield fruit in its season.
You have no fear of drought.

Who can fathom the devious perversity of the heart?
I probe the heart, and search the mind,
and allow you to reap what you sow.[3]

—JEREMIAH 17:5–10

1 God is not bound by time or space, but embraces and transcends both. There is no place devoid of God, and therefore no place in which turning cannot happen.

2 Where do you hide from God? Where do you imagine you are free to dream your dreams without having to measure them against reality?

3 Heaven and earth are embraced by God in the same way a wave is embraced by the ocean. There is no duality, only more and less inclusive understandings of nonduality.

4 Everyone dreams, and your dreams always place the small self at the center. Even a nightmare has you in the starring role. The prophet is never the point, and always the pointer.

5 Don't imagine that God's word is always soothing. There are times when the only way to wake up is with a shout of alarm. The dire predictions of the prophets are not portraits of what must be, but only sketches of what will be if you do not return to your true nature and take up the way of justice, compassion, and humility.

The One Who Is says:

Am I God only to those nearby,
and not those far away?[1]
If you go into hiding, do I not see you?[2]
I embrace heaven and earth.[3]
I have heard the false prophets prophesy in
My name, saying,
"I had a dream! I had a dream!"
They dream only of their own deceitful desire,
and hope to make you forget My Name in favor
of their dreams....
The one with My word speaks truth ...[4]
My word is like fire, like a hammer shattering rock.[5]

—JEREMIAH 23:23–29

1 What is God's listening? It is God fully present to you in, as, and at this very moment. God is always present. The question is: Are you?

2 A whole heart is a heart that holds nothing back. Do not imagine you must be a certain way with God; that you must feel faithful and trusting; that you must overcome doubt, anger, and fear. Seek God through your imperfections and confusion. Without changing anything, turn your whole self to God, and let God change everything.

3 You are in captivity when having rather than being governs your life. Then you are held by the allure of things, and people are means rather than ends in themselves.

4 You are in exile when your desire to have and possess puts you in competition with other people. You imagine that they must lose if you are to win, and that compulsion to win drives you out into the world and into the egoic fantasy of your self-projected idols.

5 How can you know that which surpasses understanding? Only by dropping the narrow mind of selfish preoccupation, and recovering the spacious mind of selfless reconciliation. The secrets are open. It is you who is closed.

The One Who Is says:

I know the plans I have set for you:
plans for your welfare, not your destruction.
My desire is for a future filled with hope.

When you call Me,
when you follow Me,
when you pray to Me,
I will listen.[1]
When you seek Me you will find Me,
providing that you seek Me with a whole heart.[2]

I am available to you, and I will restore your fortunes.
I will gather you in from your places of captivity,[3]
and I will bring you home from your places of exile.[4]

Call Me, and I will answer you.
I will reveal to you wondrous things;
secrets that surpass your understanding.[5]

—JEREMIAH 33:3

1 "Even now" with all your uncertainty, all your intellectual sophistication, all your selfishness and greed—just turn, and God will embrace you.

2 Do not make an outward show of turning. Do not announce your piety with displays of self-torture. Let your heart burst; let your feelings—good and bad—have their day; and in the end, exhausted with your narrow self, you will find your spacious self and the One Who Is both.

3 Do you fear that God will punish you for your mistakes and imperfections? This is just another way to avoid turning. Do you imagine you are too wicked to be loved? This is just another way to avoid facing your true nature. God does not punish; God simply allows the consequences of your actions to play out in your life. If you don't like the output, change the input.

4 What is it you need to know in order to return? You need to know that you can return, here and now, just as you are. And the regret? That you did not do this sooner.

The One Who Is says:

Even now, turn back to Me with a whole heart,[1]
with fasting, with weeping, and with lamentation.
Rend your heart and not your garment,[2]
and return to Me.
I am gracious and kind,
patient and overflowing with compassion.
I renounce punishment.[3]
Whoever knows, let them return and regret.[4]

—JOEL 2:12

1 The prophet Jonah is sent to Nineveh to call the Gentiles to return to God. He resists, and is carried there against his will by a great fish. He speaks to the people and they turn from evil. Fearful that their action will make the unrepentant Jews seem all the more stubborn, Jonah pouts in the heat of the day. God sends a plant to give him shade, and then allows the plant to be eaten by worms. Jonah laments the loss of the plant. God uses Jonah's loss to highlight the fact that if Jonah can love a plant in which he has invested nothing, how can God not love all beings in whom God has invested everything?

Do not think that God loves only the few, or even the many. God loves all, for God is all.

The One Who Is says:

> If you can care for that which you neither
> birth nor nurture,
> how much more should I care for that
> which I did birth and continue to nurture.[1]
> —BASED ON JONAH 4:9–11

1 This is the heart of the matter. There is nothing you need bring to God, for God is everything. There is no way to the One; the way itself is the One. God does not want something from you; God wants something of you: justice, kindness, and humility.

It is so simple; why do you complicate it? It is so clear; why do you muddy it? You do these things to avoid doing the very thing God asks. You occupy yourself with theologies, and pore over ancient texts as if the menu were the meal.

Only do this: Act justly by treating all beings as manifestations of God; act kindly by putting others ahead of yourself; act humbly by returning again and again to your true self, the One Who Is all.

The prophet Micah says:

With what shall you approach the One Who Is?
How shall you humble yourself before the
Transcendent One?
Shall you seek to appease God with burnt offerings,
with yearling calves?

Would the One Who Is be appeased with
thousands of rams,
with tens of thousands of streams of oil?
Shall you give over your firstborn to atone for
your transgression,
the fruit of your belly for the error of your heart?

God has told you what is good.
What does the One Who Is require of you?
Only to do justly and to love kindness,
and to walk humbly with your God.[1]

—MICAH 6:6–9

1 Do you wish to prosper in this transient world of seemingly separate things? Do not seek to overwhelm others with armies of soldiers and strength of arms. Do not seek to impress and convince with armies of words and strength of argument. Do not seek to conscript and enlist with armies of lies and strength of flattery. Live only by the breath of God.

Living by the breath of God means attending to the moment, one breath at a time. It means being aware of the unity of inside and outside, of inhalation and exhalation, of self and other, of I and Thou. It means knowing that the world is not black or white, but black and white; not good or bad, but good and bad; not a matter of us or them, but always the interplay of us and them. It means living with the wisdom that everything is one thing, and the one thing is God.

The One Who Is says:

> Not by armies,
> nor by strength,
> but by My breath.[1]

—ZECHARIAH 4:6

1 You cannot reason with God as you would reason with another, for with God there is no other. What you can do is enter into the mind of God, realizing that the spacious mind of God already embraces and informs the narrow mind of self. What you can do is awaken to the fact that you and God are already together as one, and the truth that flows from this knowing is the truth that bleaches the dye of ignorance out of the wool of your life.

The One Who Is says:

> Do I need your endless sacrifices?
> I am stuffed with burnt offerings ...
> I cannot stand your pomp and solemnity.
> I am disgusted by your ceremonies of
> time and season....
>
> Wash yourselves clean, put away your evil acts,
> cease from doing evil, learn to do good.
> Seek justice, aid the wronged,
> defend the powerless, the orphan and the widow.
>
> Come, let us reason together.
> Even if your sins are scarlet, they can become
> snow white;
> even if they are as wool dyed crimson,
> they can be white as fleece.[1]
>
> —ISAIAH 1:11–19

1 When the truth is known, your eyes will see what they have not yet seen: the unity of all things in, with, and as God.

2 When the truth is known, your ears will hear what they have not yet heard: the silence between the sounds that allows you to perceive the symphony that was earlier mistaken for mere noise.

3 The impetuous heart, the heart panting and racing and endlessly hunting for something to satisfy its longing for eternity, cannot become wise. Wisdom comes from stillness.

4 When you know little, you speak much; and the volume of words you mumble in saying it masks the nonsense of what you say. As the heart slows into stillness, the mind quiets into silence, and the tongue is at rest. You speak only when it is warranted, and your speech is humble, just, and kind.

The One Who Is says:

> Then your eyes shall see even what seeing
> eyes did not;[1]
> then your ears will hear even what hearing
> ears did not.[2]
> Even the impetuous heart will understand wisdom,[3]
> and the mumbling tongue will speak fluently and well.[4]
> —ISAIAH 32:3–4

1 From the perspective of the whole, there is no before or after; no time and space. This is radical nonduality: There is only that ineffable reality that embraces and transcends both the one and the many. From the perspective of the part, there is before and after; time and space. The work of the part is to see what it sees in the greater context of the whole.

The understanding God asks of you is not the negation of the self, but the return of the self to the whole. The ocean makes waves, the sun shines—waves and sunlight are the ways of manifestation. They are not to be denigrated. They are simply not to be worshiped. Do not mistake the part for the whole or imagine that the whole eliminates the part. Rather, see the first and the last and everything in between as unique and precious manifestations of the One Who Is all.

The One Who Is says:

Understand that I am God;
there is no god before Me or any after Me.
I alone am the One Who Is, and there is no one
else to save you....

I am the first and I am the last,
and there is no god but Me.[1]

—ISAIAH 43:11; 44:6

1 Again Isaiah reminds you of the nonduality of God. There is nothing else but God, for if there were, then God would be limited and a limited god is not God. Can you see this? Can you look out your window and see not only the diversity of things but also the unity out of which each arises? Not the One and the many, but the One Who Is the many?

2 You want a god who is only light, only good, only love. But a god that is only anything is not the true God who is everything. If God is one thing and not its opposite, then this opposite is as great as God. God manifests all opposites, for that is what it is to be God, to be the whole. Just as a magnet needs both poles to be itself, so God needs all opposites to be God. Thus God is the source of evil, but this is not to say that God does evil. God is everything and does nothing. Doing implies volition, and God's will is only to be God, the whole that allows for the finite play of finite parts.

The One Who Is says:

> I am the One Who Is;
> there is nothing else.[1]
> Beside Me, there is no god....
> I form light and create darkness;
> I make peace and create evil —
> I the One Who Is do all these things.[2]

—Isaiah 45:5–7

1 What are the obstacles on the path? The idols of narrow self that distract you. You imagine that you need something to help you walk the path. You need nothing but the decision to walk. You think you have to be worthy. You only have to be willing. And not even that! Just walk!

2 There is no *high* without *low.* God cannot dwell on only one without also inhabiting the other. For God embraces the one and the other, and transcends them both. Do not think you must be other than you are. Simply take up the path where you find it—right beneath your feet.

The One Who Is says:

> Pave a highway! Clear a road!
> Remove all obstacles from the path!...[1]
>
> I dwell on high, in holiness;
> yet also with the contrite and the lowly in spirit—
> reviving their spirits, uplifting their hearts.[2]
> —ISAIAH 57:14–15

From Injustice...

...to Justice

1 The accumulation of evil is what condemns you, and even then it is not God's desire to punish you. The weight of your deeds simply tips the scales, making the consequences of your actions inescapable.

2 Where have you failed to be generous with the poor and impoverished? Where have you used leverage against those beneath you in rank and power? Where have you led people down blind alleys simply to get what you want? Where do you take advantage of the system's injustice, rather than reforming the system to make it more just? See the injustice you do, and cease from doing it.

The One Who Is says:

> I do not rebuke you for every offense,
> but the weight of your injustice forces My hand.[1]
> For these reasons do you suffer:[2]
> Because you bribe judges and undermine the
> claims of the just;
> because you artificially raise prices and
> impoverish the poor;
> because you trample the heads of the powerless
> into the dust;
> because you force the humble to walk a crooked path;
> because young and old are inundated with selfishness;
> because you lounge on garments the poor are
> forced to pawn;
> because you get drunk on unjust taxes…
>
> —AMOS 2:6–8

1 The clarity and simplicity of God's way is the inexorable nature of cause and effect. As you do, so it shall be done to you. Evil kills. Even if you imagine you have avoided the consequences of your actions, look again; the tension and anxiety that haunt you are killing you and any hope of lasting joy within you.

2 Actions, not intent, is the issue here. It is not the thought that counts, but the quality of the deed. You may not feel generous, yet if you act generously, your life is enriched. You may not feel wicked, but if you rob people of dignity, your life is racked with fear that the same will be done to you.

3 God calls you to turn and return: to turn from evil and do good, and to return to your true nature as a manifestation of God. These are actions, not emotions; deeds based on decisions, not dreams based on desire. You may want to turn and yet never turn. You may not feel like turning and turn nevertheless. Do not imagine that you have to feel a certain way to return to God. Do not imagine that you have to overcome some aspect of yourself, or fix something in yourself. Even guilt about the past is useless. Just turn. The turning itself will bring about the new heart and the new spirit.

The One Who Is says:

You say, "The way of God is unfair."
But it isn't My way that is unfair, but yours.
My way is clear: Act and be acted upon in kind.[1]
When you turn away from righteousness and do evil,
you shall die for it; your own evil shall kill you.
When you turn your back on evil and do
what is just and right,
your turning shall save you....

So do not claim My way is unfair....
I judge you according to your deeds.[2]
Return to goodness and turn away from evil;
do not dwell upon past error
or let guilt become a stumbling block for you.[3]
Cast the past aside and make for yourself a new heart
and a new spirit.
Why die from old errors?
I do not desire death ... turn back and live!
—EZEKIEL 18:25–32

1   You may be tempted to dismiss this attack as hyperbole. Don't. Think instead of how Habakkuk may be speaking truth in the face of your denial. To what extent has your pursuit of wealth or fame been a detriment to your relationships with loved ones? Where have you advanced your career or position in the community at the expense of others? Where have you exploited another's weakness for your own gain?

You are not the only one to do these things. Do not imagine you are the only one to avoid doing them. Rather, look honestly at your life, see where you participate in injustice, and turn.

The One Who Is says:

Your wealth is acquired at the expense of your family.
You build your nest high atop the bodies
of the exploited.
Your plans shame your own house,
and bring guilt on your own head....

You get others drunk only to gaze on their nakedness,
such is the power of your hatred.
But you will be filled with shame rather than glory,
for it is yourself you hate most of all....[1]
—HABAKKUK 2:9–16

1 Do not begin with kindness. Begin with justice. Why? When you begin with kindness, you may be swayed by the perceived suffering of others, and be blind to the causes of their suffering. You may spend all your efforts alleviating the symptom and have no energy left to root out the cause that continues to give rise to that symptom.

2 God is everywhere all the time, so where can you seek? Seeking, searching, questing are all ways to postpone awakening. Yet knowing this without knowing God leads not to awakening but to complacency. You have to seek until you know in your gut that there is no place to look. You have to quest until you realize there is no place to go. This is the paradox of the spiritual quest: You do the unnecessary until you know it is unnecessary; and then you stop. And when you stop, God is there to teach you.

3 It is God who teaches you, not a prophet, a cleric, or a guru. How does God teach you? By presenting you with things to be done moment to moment. God is what is happening. If a friend calls with some urgent favor, it is God teaching you. How will you respond? The principle of response is called *Hineini*, Here I am. This is what God wants of you: to respond to each moment with the simplicity of your presence. You cannot know in advance what God will ask of you. You can only know that the way of response is total: *Hineini*, Here I am.

The One Who Is says:

> Sow justice and reap compassion....[1]
> Make time to seek Me,[2]
> and I will come and teach you the way of
> righteousness.[3]
> But ...
> Sow wickedness and reap iniquity,
> and you will gag on the fruit of treachery.
> —HOSEA 10:12–13

1 You forsake God when you let your feelings dictate your behavior,
   Digging for yourself cisterns of shallow emotion.
You forsake God when you let fantasy blind you to reality,
   Digging for yourself cisterns of false hope.
You forsake God when you imagine some thing will make you happy,
   Digging for yourself cisterns of empty materialism.
You forsake God when you imagine some relationship will make you
   whole,
   Digging for yourself cisterns of broken hearts.
You forsake God when you hide from your pain through alcohol, drugs,
   sex, or food,
   Digging for yourself cisterns of suffering and denial.
You forsake God when you pretend you are in control of your life,
   Digging for yourself cisterns of exploitation.
You forsake God when you pretend you are not in control of your behavior,
   Digging for yourself cisterns of weak excuses.
You forsake God every time you place self before others,
   Digging for yourself cisterns of selfishness.
So ask yourself: Where do you forsake the One Who Is?

The One Who Is says:

You commit two errors:
First, you forsake Me, the Source of living waters.
Second, you dig for yourselves broken cisterns
that cannot hold water....[1]

—JEREMIAH 2:13

1 How is it you are not ashamed of your life? What have you told yourself about life that allows you to live so accustomed to denial and lies that you cannot even fathom the truth of the prophet's challenge? How have you excused your mistakes, covered up your indiscretions, hidden your hunger, and made yourself presentable to those you love and those you use? These are hard questions to ask, and harder still to answer. Do you dare?

2 What are the many roads before you? Which are timely and which are timeless? Which lead to temporary gain and which to true happiness and tranquility? It may be hard to know this at first. You may have to walk many dead ends before learning how to discern which path is right for you. But it can be done. You are forever at a crossroads. You need never walk back the way you came. You need only turn in the direction you need to go.

3 But you say, "I will not." Why do you make this so complicated? Why do you imagine it so much more difficult than it already is? Why do you rob yourself of happiness and peace? And why are you more prone to answering these questions than you are to turning—right now—to their resolution?

The One Who Is says:

From the least to the greatest, greed rules;
priest and prophet alike act falsely.
You make light of the violence around you, crying,
"Peace! Peace!"
when there is no peace.
You act shamefully and yet feel no shame.
Your cheeks never blush....[1]

Consider the many roads before you;[2]
inquire about the timeless path,
the way to happiness.
Travel this road, and find tranquility for yourself.
But you say, "I will not."[3]

—JEREMIAH 6:13–16

1 God is not hiding from you. God is hidden from you—hidden by your own delusions, indiscretions, sins, and errors. God is not ashamed of you. God is not avoiding you. God is right here, right now, holding out arms to embrace you in love and forgiveness. It is just that you cannot see God. All you can see is your own failure, your own unworthiness. This depression is false; it is yet another manifestation of your own self-importance. You imagine that somehow you are great enough to be unworthy of God's love. Even your guilt is a measure of your grandiosity. Drop both and embrace the One Who Is in the very imperfection of your life.

The One Who Is says:

> One day you will cry out to Me,
> and I will not answer.
> You will look for Me
> but My Face will be obscured,
> hidden from view by the wrongs you have done.[1]

—MICAH 3:4

From Injustice...
...to Justice

1 It is not that God hates ritual. It is that God hates ritual done without a whole heart. When you pretend to act for God but are in fact acting for self, alignment with God is impossible. So much religion is simply pretend piety, masking selfishness in the garb of selflessness. You lay claim to an exclusive revelation; you uphold salvation only for those who think as you think; you deny the unconditional love of God and offer yourself and the world an idol supportive only of your own ego and its pretensions to power.

2 God does not care about your pretensions. God wants justice. God wants righteousness. God wants you to see yourself and every other as part of the One Who Is all; and then to act from that seeing.

The One Who Is says:

> I hate your holy days
> and despise your festivals;
> I am not moved by your solemn gatherings.
> Your offerings are rejected;
> I ignore your slaughtered gifts.
> Spare me the sound of your hymns,
> and let the music of your lutes fall silent;
> I am not listening.[1]
>
> Rather let justice well up like water,
> let righteousness flow like a mighty stream.[2]

—AMOS 5:21–24

1 Desire is to God as grain is to wood, and current is to ocean. It is the way God is God. What is the grain of God? Acts of justice, kindness, and humility. This is what God desires.

2 God does not punish or reward; God simply allows the consequences of your actions to play out in your life. You reap what you sow.

3 *Teshuvah,* the power to turn from evil and do good, is at the heart of the prophetic message. This is what God desires: that you not fight the current, but surrender to it. The current is holiness, goodness. You can act otherwise, but the prophets remind you that no matter how much of a habit evil has become, you always have the power to turn from it and do good.

4 The prophets are not promising you eternal life. They are offering you a chance to avoid premature death. And do not imagine that this is just physical death. The way of the foolish and the wicked is deadening. It numbs the heart, drives out hope, and besieges you with despair. This is a death no less deadly than the cessation of breathing.

The One Who Is says:

It is not My desire[1] that you die,
but that you turn from evil and live.[2]
Turn back,[3]
turn back from your evil ways,
that you may not die…![4]

—EZEKIEL 33:11

1 The dwelling place God promises you is the place you happen to be at this and every moment. When you act unjustly, cruelly, selfishly, you do not dwell anywhere, for you are forever running from one place to another in hopes of escaping the consequences of your deeds. But if you act justly, kindly, and selflessly, you need not run, but can dwell in the moment without fear, and appreciate the love and peace that is there when you are doing good.

2 This is what Jesus said to the priests as he drove the moneychangers out of the Temple. The Temple had become the center of economic as well as religious power, and a thriving trade in sacrificial animals brought with it moneychangers who could facilitate the purchase of animals by people coming to Jerusalem from elsewhere. These were businesspeople not thieves. The thieves are those who rob the people of truth by teaching them that deeds don't matter, and that they can buy their way out of distress and into God's grace. God's grace is never bought or earned; it is simply turned to and embraced. The lie of the Temple, the lie of religion, is that you need a mediator between you and God, when all you really need is to turn.

The One Who Is says:

> If you really mend your ways and your actions;
> if you execute justice between you and others;
> if you cease oppressing the stranger, the orphan,
> and the widow;
> if you stop shedding the blood of the innocent;
> if you abandon your harmful devotion to other gods,
> then will I allow you to dwell in this place....[1]

> You trust in the illusion that you can
> steal, murder, fornicate, lie, and worship false gods,
> and then come and stand before Me ... and say
> "We are saved"...
> Do you consider My House to be a den of thieves?[2]
> —JEREMIAH 7:5–11

1 This is what God desires: kindness, mercy, and justice to the powerful and the powerless alike. Everything else is mere distraction.

The One Who Is says:

> Execute true justice;
> deal kindly and compassionately with one another.
> Do not oppress the widow,
> the orphan, the stranger, and the poor.
> Do not set your heart to plotting evil.[1]
>
> —ZECHARIAH 7:8–10

1 God is present to you only when you are present to God. Being present to God means seeing all beings as manifestations of the One Being, and treating them with the utmost respect and care. Your pious acts are meaningless if they do not lead you to this recognition of God in all as all. Before you rush off to meet some religious obligation, look first to your obligations to God: caring for those in need. Do this and God will be present to you. Do otherwise and you will find nothing but hollow words and empty deeds.

The One Who Is says:

You ask Me: "When I fast, why do You ignore me?
I starved myself, and You paid me no attention."
I will tell you why:
Because you fast for personal gain, and oppress
all your laborers!
Because you fast and yet continue to sow strife
and violence …
Your fast has nothing to do with what I desire …
This is the fast I desire:
to break open the shackles of wickedness;
to untie the cords of injustice;
to free the oppressed and put an end to evil.
To share your bread with the hungry;
to house the homeless in your homes;
to clothe the naked; and not ignore the
needy among you.
Then your light shall burst through like dawn,
and your healing will swiftly spring up …
Then, when you call, I will answer;
When you cry, I will say: Here I am.[1]

—ISAIAH 58:3–9

1 The Sabbath is a day for living as God intended you to live: not scrabbling for a living, but delighting in life. The Sabbath is a day for practicing selflessness, humility, mercy, and justice. It is a day of mindfulness, when the distractions of the week are set aside that you might see the One Who Is as all that is. Six days a week you project yourself on others, blinding yourself to the true self you all share. But on the Sabbath you withdraw from your projects and see what is: God. On the Sabbath you return to truth, so that when the workweek comes around once more, you engage it with a bit more wisdom than you had the week before.

The One Who Is says:

If you refrain from trampling the Sabbath,
if you set aside My holy day and free yourself
from chasing profit;
if you call the Sabbath a "delight" and an "honor";
if you cherish it by setting aside your own affairs
by not pursuing money,
by not discussing business,
then you can delight in Me.[1]

—ISAIAH 58:13–14

From Despair...
...to Joy

1 Every seven years the land is allowed to lie fallow. Crops are not planted or harvested, and foodstuffs can become a little scarce. This is a time for generosity, not hoarding. Where do you take advantage of scarcity and another's hunger?

2 Your deepest hunger is for the Word of God. Not the word printed on a page or even spoken from a pulpit; but the Word spoken directly to you by the One Who Is, in the immediacy of your everyday life. The Word of God is the world as it presents itself to you in all its unmediated wonder. If you see the world as it is, you see God present in, with, and as all things.

3 When you are deaf to the world as Word, you begin a frantic search for that which is always with you. You cannot find it because you already have it. You starve in the midst of plenty; you thirst even as you sit beside the river. You are desolate and alone in the center of the One Who Is all. How sad. Your despair is the result of your ignorance.

The One Who Is says:

Listen to Me, you devourers of the needy,
murderers of the poor!...
You withhold produce from market to force
the prices to rise;
you hoard crops during the Sabbatical year;[1]
you rig your scales and doctor your measures;
you sell chaff as wheat and gouge the poor
with unfair prices;
you impoverish the needy for the price of sandals.
I will never forget your actions....

Days are coming when I will cause this land
to be famished;
you will starve but not for bread,
you will thirst but not for water.
You will starve and thirst for My word.[2]
You will wander from sea to sea,
from north to east in search of My word,
but you will not find it.[3]

—Amos 8:4–12

1 God never repeats. Each moment is its own truth; it comes and goes and does not return.

2 Devouring your children is destroying your future. Devouring your parents is robbing yourself of your past. You devour the future by living a life of projection. You devour the past by living a life of imitation. The present is neither imitative nor anticipatory. It is simply itself: unique, unreplicatable, and wondrous. Despair feeds off imitation and projection.

3 God shows no pity because pity implies helplessness. You are not helpless. You are simply attached to your imitations and projections. God's compassion is in the despair itself. It is only when your suffering is great enough that you will finally drop the idols of self that govern your life, and open your eyes to the One Who Is.

The One Who Is says:

>Your wickedness brings this upon you.
>I will do among you what I have never done before
>and will never do again.[1]
>Parents will eat their children,
>and children will devour their parents,[2]
>and I will scatter you in every direction....
>I will show you no pity....[3]
>—EZEKIEL 5:9–11

1 The Day of Despair is as close as your delusional thinking. You can taste the gathering soot every time you engage in injustice and cruelty. It fills your belly with dread; for if you can do this to others, there will be others who will do this to you. Your own actions stoke the flames of your personal hell.

2 The first fire is the one you set with thoughtless and selfish actions. The second fire is the one this first fire begets by inviting others to do the same. Do not imagine that your actions are limited. They are pebbles tossed into a pond: Their ripples will expand everywhere.

3 Nothing can escape the despair you set in motion. It will infect your life and the lives of everyone you love and come in contact with. Even your most fertile connections will dry up and die, because you cannot water them with the emotional wasteland you are becoming.

The One Who Is says:

> Blow the shofar in Zion,
> sound the alarm on My holy mount!
> Let all those who dwell on earth tremble,
> for My day is close.[1]
>
> A day, gloomy and dark;
> a day of choking fog spread over the hills
> like a blanket of soot ...
>
> A fire shall sweep the earth before the gloom
> and another shall follow after it.[2]
> What was once fertile as Eden
> will be left desolate and waste.
> Nothing shall escape.[3]

—JOEL 2:1–3

1 In the wake of the destruction of all you have built for yourself, there is a transformation. God's breath will return to you. You will begin to sense the stirrings of truth within you. Dreams, visions, and prophecies will come to you from within and without. But they will be wonders not yet healing in nature. They will reveal to you the truth that your last hope of escaping the worst is false. You will hit the wall of abject helplessness at last.

2 Only when all hope is dashed; only when the self has tasted its own powerlessness; only when the idols of selfishness have been shown to be hollow and weak; only then will you call out to God from the simple fact of your own brokenness, and when you do, the refuge is open, and you will live.

The One Who Is says:

> After the destruction, I will breathe My spirit
> into all flesh;
> your sons and daughters will prophesy;
> the aged will dream prophetic dreams,
> and the young will see visions.
> I will pour out My spirit
> even upon your slaves and servants.[1]
> The sky and the earth will be filled with wonders:
> dark red flames and pillars of smoke;
> the sun will go black and the moon turn blood red …
> But anyone who calls out My name will escape,
> for I will set a refuge on Mount Zion and
> in Jerusalem …
> and any who call upon Me will survive.[2]
>
> —JOEL 3:1–5

1 Do not trust anyone to save you. Do not burden another, even the most beloved, with your salvation. This is your task alone.

2 If you seek to find solace in your household, both people and possessions, they will become the enemies of your salvation. They will become idols for you, means to an end they cannot deliver. You will exploit their love, even as you declare that they have no love for you. You will pervert their compassion into sympathy, and their sympathy into pity, and you will despise them for even looking at you.

3 There is nothing you can do to save yourself. Nothing but wait. Waiting is key. To wait for God is to trust in God. Trusting means waiting in the midst of not-knowing. If you wait long enough, your mind will quiet its self-loathing, and you will hear what is being whispered to you each moment of your life: "Fear not. I am with you."

The prophet Micah says:

> [At the Day of Judgment] trust no one,
> not even a friend,
> not even your lover.[1]
> Be guarded in speech,
> even with your children.
> For sons will turn against fathers,
> and daughters will rise up against mothers,
> and in-laws against each other.
> You own household will become your enemy.[2]
>
> Put your trust in the One Who Is,
> and wait for the God of your redemption.[3]
> God will hear you.

—MICAH 7:5–7

1 The Day of Judgment is the day you succumb to despair. It is the day your warrior self, the proud self-reliant you that takes what it wants by overwhelming others, faces a foe greater than itself. It is the day all your defenses tumble; all your fantasies crash. This is a day of horror, and it is absolutely necessary. Until everything false crumbles, you will always be blind to the real.

The prophet Zephaniah says:

> The great Day of Judgment is near,
> and nearer still.
> This will be a bitter day.
> A day when warriors shriek in fear;
> a day of fury;
> a day of trouble and distress;
> a day of disaster and desolation;
> a day of thick fog and black clouds;
> a day of clashing armies, fallen cities,
> and crumbling towers.[1]
>
> —ZEPHANIAH 1:14–16

1 Do not imagine that the desolation that is coming is a punishment upon the innocent. It is simply and horribly the consequence of the quality of your own actions. You were made for justice, and chose injustice. You were made for compassion, and chose cruelty. You were made for humility, and chose hubris. You were made sweet, and chose to be sour. Do not blame God for your actions. If you stick your finger into an electrical socket, do you blame electricity for the shock you receive? Reap what you sow: It is the only way to face the decision to turn.

The prophet Isaiah says:

My Beloved had a vineyard on a fertile hill.
My Beloved fenced it around and cleared it of stones,
planted it with choice vines, and built
a watchtower inside.
My Beloved hewed within it a wine press and hoped
it would yield fine grapes,
but bitter grapes were the only harvest ...
[My Beloved said:]
"So let me tell you what I plan for my vineyard.
I will flatten the fence and break down the watchtower.
It will let it be ravaged and trampled.
I will allow it to become desolate...."

You are the vineyard of the One Who Is.
You are the seedling so tenderly planted.
From you God hoped for justice,
but you brought forth only wickedness.
God hoped for mercy and you offered only cruelty.[1]

—Isaiah 5:1–7

1 There is no escape from the ambush of your own cruelty and misdeeds. But there is a response: Howl. Howling is a raw expression of your pain, horror, and fear. It is an inarticulate yet definite blast of truth. You are reduced to primal emotion, and nothing makes sense.

When you howl, you release the energies building up within you. When you howl, you shatter the façade of denial and the delusion that there is rescue waiting. When you howl, you cease all thought and feeling, and reach a level of sheer being that is beneath the foundation of self. When you howl, you exhaust the last remnants of hope, and collapse into a helpless heap. It is only there that you will find the strength you need to rise again.

The prophet Isaiah says:

Howl! Judgment Day is near; it comes like an ambush.
Your hands will grow limp, and your heart will melt,
overcome by terror.
You will have seizures,
and cramps like women in labor.
You will see your friends and recoil in horror:
their faces aflame with fear....

Your babies will be dashed before your eyes.
Your home will be plundered,
you will be raped,
and your children shot through with arrows....[1]
—ISAIAH 13:6–17

1 Despair is a closed system; entropy rules; there is no escape. Your sense of terror at the coming dread will motivate your scheming to a feverish level. You will plot ways of avoiding the consequences of your acts, but these plots too will condemn you. Wherever you run, there will be the pit of despair. If you climb out and seek a high place of detachment, the detachment itself will ensnare you in a lifeless world without love or hope. There is no exit. What should you do? Wait and allow the horror to unfold around and within you. The day of destruction is also a day of cleansing. If you can sit through it, it will all pass and leave in its wake a new day of uncompromising promise.

The prophet Isaiah says:

> This is what awaits you if you continue your
> commitment to evil:
> terror, the pit, and the snare!
> If you run at the report of terror, you will
> fall into the pit.
> If you manage to climb out of the pit,
> you shall become ensnared in the trap.[1]
> —ISAIAH 24:17–18

1 Seek refuge *in* God, not *with* God. Do not continue the delusion that God is other than you, or that you are separate from God. Do not resist God's anger. Do not pretend you can douse God's fire. Surrender to what is as what must be, given the conditions you have set in motion.

Taking refuge in God means taking no action and fueling no consequence. It means allowing the fires of the past to burn themselves out in the present. You will be burned—make no mistake. You will be pained; there is no escape. But sit and wait and know in whom you dwell, and the suffering will pass. Despair will give way to joy, if you will allow it.

The prophet Nahum says:

> The One Who Is is passionate and vengeful.
> The One Who Is is fierce, and rages against foes.
>
> The One Who Is is patient, but not infinitely so.
> God's path is a tornado, a hurricane; clouds are the
> dust of God's feet....
>
> Who can stand before the fury of God?
> Who can resist the wrath of God?
> The anger of the One Who Is pours out like fire,
> and rocks shatter because of the Divine.
> The One Who Is is good to those who hope
> in the Divine,
> a refuge in times of distress.
> The One Who Is is mindful of those
> who seek refuge in the Divine.[1]
> —NAHUM 1:1–7

From Despair...
...to Joy

1 The earth will be so fertile that harvests will last well into the planting seasons.

2 God restores you when you return to your true nature. Your turning and your restoration are one in the same. The decision to turn frees you from the delusion of your separateness from God. Without that delusion, you are attuned to and in touch with godliness.

3 What is "your land"? From a historical perspective, the land is the Promised Land of Israel. From a personal spiritual perspective, the land is this very moment. You are uprooted from the land when you are caught up in your own psychological drama, drawing from the past, projecting onto the future, and cut off from the only place God can be met: the present moment.

The One Who Is says:

Days are coming when your bounty is so great
that the season for plowing will overlap the season
for reaping;[1]
when the pressing of grapes will overlap the planting
of new seed;
when the mountains shall drip wine
and all the hills shall wave with grain.

I will restore you....[2]

I will plant you upon your land,
and never again shall you be uprooted from it....[3]

—Amos 9:13–15

1 What is this new heart? It is a heart undefended, fearless; open to the suffering of others without hiding in the drama of self. It is the awakened heart that allows the full range of feelings to wash over you without your being blown away by them.

2 What is this new breath? It is your next breath, if you would but awaken to the One Who Is here, now, and always.

3 You follow God best from the inside out. Each breath brings you into the present moment. Each breath is an opportunity to know the One Who Is as what is happening in, with, and around you. With this knowing comes the way of God, the way of justice, compassion, and humility—not as rules imposed from without, but as a subtle truth informing you from within.

The One Who Is says:

I will give you a new heart[1]
and put new breath into you:[2]
I will remove the heart of stone from your body,
and give you a heart of flesh.

I will put My breath into you,
and in this way you will follow all My decrees
and faithfully observe My ordinances.[3]

—EZEKIEL 36:26–28

1 In one sentence Haggai summarizes the message of the prophets: God is with you. How might you understand the nearness of God? Listen to what God says in Deuteronomy:

> It is not in the sky, that you should say, "Who among us can go up to the heavens and get it for us and teach it to us, that we may observe it?" Neither is it beyond the sea, that you should say, "Who among us can cross the ocean and get it for us and impart it to us, that we may observe it?" No, the thing is very close to you, in your mouth and in your heart, to observe it (Deuteronomy 30:12–14).

The "thing" is the way of godliness. It is in your mouth, that your speech be healing rather than hurtful. It is in your heart, that you nurture compassion rather than hatred. And by turning your lips and your heart to holiness, you observe the way and walk it. When you walk in the way of God, you walk with the awareness that God is with you, in you, is you. This is what the prophets are telling you: The way is near; turn to it, and be healed.

The One Who Is says:

I am with you.[1]

—HAGGAI 1:13

1   Do not imagine that this new breath is different from your last breath or your next breath. It is this breath, now, and now again. And when you know the truth of God breathing within you, you know the truth of your unity with God, in God, as God. You are no longer alone; no longer a stranger. You are the One Who Is and you are at one with all. And with this knowing comes a liberation from fear that makes you at last ready for love.

The One Who Is says:

My breath is always within you.
Fear not![1]

—HAGGAI 2:5

1 To be God's woman or man, you have to awaken to the inner teaching of justice, kindness, and humility. You have to feel not commanded but compelled to do what is right. How do you awaken to this inner Torah? By turning from selfishness to selflessness; by doing justly; by loving mercy; by walking humbly with God manifest as all things.

2 Teachers and their teachings are to God what a menu is to a meal. They point to something other than themselves. When the meal is served, of what use is the menu? Put it aside and eat. Taste for yourself and see the nature of God manifest in and as all things—including yourself.

The One Who Is says:

> Days are coming when I will seal a new
> covenant with you.
> It will be a different covenant than that
> which I made with your ancestors....
>
> This is the covenant I will make with you:
> I shall place My Torah within you;
> I will write My Teaching on your heart;
> then I will be your God and you will be My child.[1]
>
> Then you will no longer need
> teachers and sages urging you to know Me,
> for you shall know Me naturally;[2]
> from the smallest among you to the greatest,
> all will know Me.
> And I will forgive you all your errors,
> and let fade all memory of your wickedness.
>
> —JEREMIAH 31:30–34

1 This is your place, this place you happen to be at just this moment. When God returns you to your place, you are not moved from one spot to another, but are suddenly aware that this spot was the very spot for which you have been searching all your life.

2 The security of the awakened heart is the surety that all things change, and that there is nothing that need be done about it.

3 Until this awakening occurs, you are not yet part of God's people, nor is God truly your God. Until this awakening, you continue to worship the idol of self, the gods of power, control, and permanence. It is only when your gods fail you, only when you are crushed beneath the weight of your own ignorance, injustice, and cruelty, that you can see the invalid nature of your idols and turn to God, the One Who Is the turning itself.

The One Who Is says:

> I will return you to your place,[1]
> and cause you to dwell securely.[2]
> You shall be Mine and I will be yours.[3]
>
> I will give you a single heart and a single path:
> awe of Me;
> and in this way will things be well with you
> and your children.

—JEREMIAH 32:37–39

1 Fear drives out joy and invites shame. Awakening to your true self, you have no need to be afraid. Without fear there is no shame. There is only the humble acceptance of your deeds and their consequences. And because you realize that the one begets the other, you are careful to do well by yourself and others so as to set in motion a healing future and not a hurtful one.

The One Who Is says:

> Earth! Don't be afraid;
> rejoice and be glad....
>
> Beasts! Don't be afraid;
> the pastures are once again clothed with sweet grass.
> The trees are fruitful; fig tree and vine are
> laden with fruit.
>
> Humans! Be glad and rejoice!
> The One Who Is has given you teachers
> of righteousness
> and has brought the rains in their season,
> early and late;
> your granaries are piled high with grain;
> your barrels overflow with wine and oil....
>
> You will eat your fill ...
> and you shall know that I am in your midst;
> that I am the One Who Is
> and there is nothing else.
> And you will never be ashamed again.[1]
>
> —JOEL 2:21–27

1   Even if you are not yet awake, know that awakening awaits you. This hope is the promise God makes to you personally. It is rooted in the fact of your unity with God. It is not that someday you will be different than you are now. It is that someday—this day—you will discover who you really are and have been since the beginning.

2   Zion is both the land of Israel and the land beneath your feet when you are awake to the fact that the whole earth is filled with God. Jerusalem is the capital of Israel, and also *Yiru Shalem,* the City of Peace and Wholeness that reveals itself to you when you are whole and at peace. Torah is the teaching that flows from being aligned with the holiness of place and the wholeness of heart.

3   War doesn't come naturally to people; it must be taught and learned. When the learning ceases, when we are no longer taught to hate the stranger, the natural compassion of human for human arises spontaneously.

4   Fear is the killer, and fearlessness the mark of the awake and aware human being.

5   The unity of humankind envisioned by the prophets is a unity through diversity. Your uniqueness will be valued as the means by which God explores the endless facets of embodied existence.

The One Who Is says:

In the days to come ...[1]

Torah shall go forth from Zion,
the word of the One Who Is from Jerusalem ...[2]

You will beat your swords into plowshares and
your spears into pruning knives.
Nation will not lift up sword against nation;
nor will you study war any more.[3]

Rather you will sit
under your vine
and your fig tree,
and be unafraid.[4]

For it is I, the One Who Is, who speaks.
Though you will walk your own path,
you will still walk to Me,
the One Who Is throughout time and eternity.[5]

—MICAH 4:1–5

[1] The little child is you at your simplest and most spiritual. In a similar vein, Jesus taught that until you become like little children you cannot enter the Kingdom of Heaven. The idea is to be like a child and not a child once more. That is, you are to regain the open-hearted curiosity of the child, and it is this childlike wonder and amazement at life that will reveal to you the divine nature of living.

[2] Violence and fear are at the root of the deluded and delusional world imagined by the small self. These are totally absent when you awaken to God as the One Who Is.

The One Who Is says:

>The wolf will live with the lamb;
>the leopard lie down with the kid;
>the calf, the lion cub, and the fatling will walk together,
>and a little child will lead them.[1]

>The cow and the bear shall graze the same pasture,
>and their young shall lie down together;
>and the lion, like the ox, shall eat straw.
>A baby will play over a viper's hole,
>and an infant pass his hand over an adder's den.

>In all of My sacred mount there shall be no evil
>or injury;
>for the earth shall be as filled with devotion to Me
>as the ocean is covered with the water of the sea.[2]

—Isaiah 11:6–9

1 Your hunger for material goods was driven by your urge to fill a void you imagined within you. When you awaken to God, the void is seen as illusory. You lack nothing and need little. You live simply, not by choice, but by design. It is not that you choose to rein in your desires, but that without the false hunger driving you, you discover that you no longer have those desires at all.

2 God is all, and everything will teach you.

3 Your deviation will spark the hearing, just as smoke sets off a smoke alarm. It is immediate and strong. The way of God is straight and is walked without wobbling. Tipping right or left suggests a drunkenness of the self on selfishness, and is quietly corrected so that the despair and destruction of the past need never be repeated. This does not mean that you will not stumble on the path, but only that you will pick yourself up quickly and return to the way.

The prophet Isaiah says:

> The One Who Is will see to your needs,
> though you will need little.[1]
> You will see beyond the material,
> the Teacher will no longer be obscured from view,
> and you will see your Teacher clearly.[2]
>
> And if you wander from the Path,
> either to the right or to the left,
> your ears will hear and you will heed the counsel:
> "This is the path, walk it."[3]

—ISAIAH 30:20–21

1 The new heaven and new earth are simply the old heaven and the old earth seen with new eyes. Do not imagine that the world is other than it was. Rather, be aware that you are seeing it as it is for the first time.

2 Joy and delight rather than fear and shame are the hallmarks of the awakened soul. This is how you know that you are on the right path. If each step brings joy to you and others; if each step is a delight to self and stranger; if your every step is peaceful, gentle, just, and kind, then you are on the Path. If not, then not. Return once more.

3 When you awaken to God as the One Who Is all that is, you no longer imagine yourself on a spiritual quest or search. You have and are all you need. Your prayer and the answer to your prayer are one: connection to God. Your request and the answer to your request are one: alignment with God. Each step is the first step. Each step is the last step. There is nowhere to go. You have arrived without going anywhere.

The One Who Is says:

Behold!
I am creating a new heaven and a new earth....[1]
Rejoice and be happy forever in what I am creating.
For I shall create Jerusalem as joy, and her
people as delight....[2]

Even before you pray,
I will answer;
even as you ask,
I will respond.[3]

—Isaiah 65:17–24

Afterword ☐

In the introduction to his monumental study of the Hebrew prophets, Abraham Joshua Heschel, one of the most profound Jewish philosophers of the twentieth century, offers this insight into the nature of the prophetic task: "The prophet was an individual who said 'No' to his society, condemning its habits and assumptions, its complacency, waywardness, and syncretism.... His fundamental objective was to reconcile man and God."[1]

Throughout this book you have been confronted by the prophetic challenge: Turn from ignorance to truth, from injustice to justice, from despair to joy, and in so doing reconcile yourself with God. What does *reconciliation* mean? First let me tell you what it cannot mean. It cannot mean that you are bridging a gap between you and God. There is no gap; you cannot be separate from God, because you cannot be other than God. God is the One Who Is; God is the one reality that manifests as all things. You are God the way a wave is the ocean. There is no reconciliation of wave and ocean; the unity is a priori and absolute.

Unlike the wave, however, you can imagine that you are other than the ocean, and in so doing place yourself in opposition to both the ocean and your fellow waves. The "you" that pretends to separateness is *mochin d'katnut,* the narrow mind, the ego, what Heschel calls the sovereign self. The problem is not that you have a sense of self, but that you allow that sense of self to become sovereign over you and thus blind you to seeing the world from the perspective of *mochin d'gadlut,* the spacious self, the greater self that knows itself and all selves to be a manifestation of God.

The proper role of the small self is to celebrate the preciousness of God's manifestations; to realize that

> Every person born into this world represents something new, something that never existed before, something original and unique. It is every man's duty to know and consider that he is unique in the world in his particular character and that there has never been someone like him in the world, for if there has been someone like him, there would have been no need for him to be in the world. Every single man is a new thing in the world, and is called upon to fulfill his particularity in this world…. Every man's foremost task is the actualization of his unique, unprecedented and never-recurring potentialities, and not the repetition of something that another, be it even the greatest, has already achieved.[2]

When the ego functions as it should, it realizes its "unique, unprecedented and never-recurring potentialities" and seeks to actualize them. The problem arises when it fails to realize two further truths. First, that others are equally unique, unprecedented, and never-recurring, and therefore due the same degree of respect that the ego seeks for itself. Second, that uniqueness is not indicative of isolation, that the self can be unique even as it is part of the greater oneness that is God.

Without realizing these additional truths, the small self begins to exaggerate its sense of separateness. It no longer sees itself as a functional necessity and relative truth, and begins to see itself as the only, absolute, and sovereign self. This delusion of the narrow self gives rise to the need for reconciliation with God.

The need for reconciliation, then, stems not from any ontological separation, but from a psychological delusion. This delusion pushes you from self to selfishness, and leads to acts so unjust, cruel, and exploitative that society itself may collapse beneath their weight.

How does reconciliation happen? By turning from ignorance to truth, from injustice to justice, and from despair to joy. Yet if God is the One Who Is, if God is everything, how can we speak of truth being better than ignorance, or justice being better than injustice, or joy superior to despair?

The answer is found in the difference between God and godliness. God is the One Who Is, the Source and Substance of all reality. All things and their opposite are equally God, but not equally godly. Godliness is the way to realizing God in and through your unique self. Actions that lead to the realization of unity through diversity, that reveal the many as part of the One, are godly; those that lead toward separateness and isolation are ungodly. To once more utilize the metaphor of the ocean and the wave, God is the ocean; godliness is the current of the ocean. While it is true that you cannot be separate from God, it is also true that you can swim in opposition to godliness.

When you are reconciled with God, you are aligned with godliness; that is to say, when you awaken to your unity with the One Who Is, you are moved to act justly, compassionately, and humbly. Your ego takes its rightful place as a vehicle for justice, compassion, and humility. It is no longer willful but willing.

Living in accord with godliness is a choice you must make moment to moment. The prophets urge you to choose wisely, and, when you have chosen poorly, to face the consequences of your choice, turn from evil, and do good. The prophets said "no" to ego's claim to sovereignty, and "yes" to justice, mercy, and humility. The prophets do not simply condemn, but offer a principled program for personal and social transformation. The program of the prophets is eloquently stated by Micah: "You know what God requires: do justly, love kindness, and walk humbly with your God" (Micah 6:8). Doing these three things is the means by which you are reconciled with God.

Notes ▢

Introduction

1. Erich Fromm, *On Being Human* (New York: Continuum, 1994), p. 97.
2. Ibid., p. 98.
3. Erich Fromm, *To Have or to Be?* (New York: Harper and Row, 1976), p. 40.
4. Ibid., p. 40.
5. Ibid., p. 49
6. Erich Fromm, *The Dogma of Christ* (New York: Holt, Rinehart and Winston, 1963), pp. 204–205.
7. Ibid., pp. 207–208.
8. Ibid., pp. 208–209.
9. Erich Fromm, *To Have or to Be?* p. 100.

Afterword

1. Abraham Joshua Heschel, *The Prophets* (New York: Perennial Classics, 2001), p. xxix.
2. Martin Buber, *The Way of Man* (Secaucus, NJ: Carol Publishing Group, 1998), p. 16.

Suggestions for Further Reading ☐

Arthur, David. *A Smooth Stone: Biblical Prophecy in Historical Perspective.* Lanham, MD: University Press of America, 2001.

Blenkinsopp, Joseph. *A History of Prophecy in Israel.* Philadelphia: Westminster Press, 1983.

Brueffmann, Walter. *The Prophetic Imagination.* Philadelphia: Fortress Press, 1978.

Buber, Martin. *The Prophetic Faith.* New York: Harper Torchbooks, 1949.

———. *The Way of Man.* Secaucus, NJ: Carol Publishing Group, 1998.

Bulluck, C. Hassell. *An Introduction to the Old Testament Prophetic Books.* Chicago: Moody Press, 1986.

Fromm, Erich. *The Dogma of Christ.* New York: Holt, Rinehart and Winston, 1963.

———. *To Have or to Be?* New York: Harper & Row, 1976.

———. *On Being Human.* New York: Continuum, 1994.

Hamilton, Edith. *Spokesmen of God.* New York: W.W. Norton, 1949.

Heschel, Abraham Joshua. *The Prophets.* New York: Perennial Classics, 2001.

McCornville, J. Gordon. *Exploring the Old Testament,* vol. 4. Downers Grove, IL: InterVarsity Press, 2002.

Pearlman, Moshe. *In the Footsteps of the Prophets.* New York: Crowell, 1975.

Podhoretz, Norman. *The Prophets.* New York: The Free Press, 2002.

Prevost, Jean-Pierre. *How to Read the Prophets.* New York: Continuum, 1997.

Rad, Gerhard von. *The Message of the Prophets.* New York: Harper & Row, 1972.

Sawyer, John. *Prophecy and the Biblical Prophets.* Oxford: Oxford University Press, 1993.

Scott, R.B.Y. *The Relevance of the Prophets.* London: Macmillan, 1968.

Wilson, Robert. *Prophecy and Society in Ancient Israel.* Philadelphia: Fortress Press, 1980.

Winward, Stephen. *A Guide to the Prophets.* Richmond, VA: John Knox Press, 1969.

About SKYLIGHT PATHS Publishing

SkyLight Paths Publishing is creating a place where people of different spiritual traditions come together for challenge and inspiration, a place where we can help each other understand the mystery that lies at the heart of our existence.

Through spirituality, our religious beliefs are increasingly becoming a part of our lives—rather than *apart* from our lives. While many of us may be more interested than ever in spiritual growth, we may be less firmly planted in traditional religion. Yet, we do want to deepen our relationship to the sacred, to learn from our own as well as from other faith traditions, and to practice in new ways.

SkyLight Paths sees both believers and seekers as a community that increasingly transcends traditional boundaries of religion and denomination—people wanting to learn from each other, *walking together, finding the way.*

We at SkyLight Paths take great care to produce beautiful books that present meaningful spiritual content in a form that reflects the art of making high quality books. Therefore, we want to acknowledge those who contributed to the production of this book.

PRODUCTION
Jenny Buono, Bernadine Dawes & Tim Holtz

EDITORIAL
Maura D. Shaw & Emily Wichland

COVER DESIGN
Walter C. Bumford III, Stockton, Massachusetts

TEXT DESIGN
Chelsea Cloeter, River Forest, Illinois

PRINTING & BINDING
Versa Press, East Peoria, Illinois

Spiritual Biography

The Life of Evelyn Underhill
An Intimate Portrait of the Groundbreaking Author of Mysticism
by *Margaret Cropper*; Foreword by *Dana Greene*

Evelyn Underhill was a passionate writer and teacher who wrote elegantly on mysticism, worship, and devotional life. This is the story of how she made her way toward spiritual maturity, from her early days of agnosticism to the years when her influence was felt throughout the world. 6 x 9, 288 pp, 5 b/w photos, Quality PB, ISBN 1-893361-70-5 **$18.95**

Zen Effects: *The Life of Alan Watts*
by *Monica Furlong*

The first and only full-length biography of one of the most charismatic spiritual leaders of the twentieth century—now back in print!

Through his widely popular books and lectures, Alan Watts (1915–1973) did more to introduce Eastern philosophy and religion to Western minds than any figure before or since. Here is the only biography of this charismatic figure, who served as Zen teacher, Anglican priest, lecturer, academic, entertainer, a leader of the San Francisco renaissance, and author of more than 30 books, including *The Way of Zen, Psychotherapy East and West* and *The Spirit of Zen.* 6 x 9, 264 pp, Quality PB, ISBN 1-893361-32-2 **$16.95**

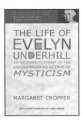 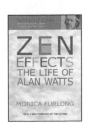 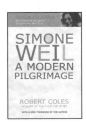 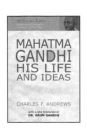

Simone Weil: *A Modern Pilgrimage*
by *Robert Coles*

The extraordinary life of the spiritual philosopher who's been called both saint and madwoman.

The French writer and philosopher Simone Weil (1906–1943) devoted her life to a search for God—while avoiding membership in organized religion. Robert Coles' intriguing study of Weil details her short, eventful life, and is an insightful portrait of the beloved and controversial thinker whose life and writings influenced many (from T. S. Eliot to Adrienne Rich to Albert Camus), and continue to inspire seekers everywhere. 6 x 9, 208 pp, Quality PB, ISBN 1-893361-34-9 **$16.95**

Mahatma Gandhi: *His Life and Ideas*
by *Charles F. Andrews*; Foreword by *Dr. Arun Gandhi*

An intimate biography of one of the greatest social and religious reformers of the modern world.

Examines from a contemporary Christian activist's point of view the religious ideas and political dynamics that influenced the birth of the peaceful resistance movement, the primary tool that Gandhi and the people of his homeland would use to gain India its freedom from British rule. An ideal introduction to the life and life's work of this great spiritual leader. 6 x 9, 336 pp, 5 b/w photos, Quality PB, ISBN 1-893361-89-6 **$18.95**

SkyLight Illuminations Series
Andrew Harvey, series editor

Offers today's spiritual seeker an enjoyable entry into the great classic texts of the world's spiritual traditions. Each classic is presented in an accessible translation, with facing pages of guided commentary from experts, giving you the keys you need to understand the history, context, and meaning of the text. This series enables readers of all backgrounds to experience and understand classic spiritual texts directly, and to make them a part of their lives. Andrew Harvey writes the foreword to each volume, an insightful, personal introduction to each classic.

Bhagavad Gita: *Annotated & Explained*
Translation by *Shri Purohit Swami;* Annotation by *Kendra Crossen Burroughs*

"The very best Gita for first-time readers." —Ken Wilber

Millions of people turn daily to India's most beloved holy book, whose universal appeal has made it popular with non-Hindus and Hindus alike. This edition introduces you to the characters, explains references and philosophical terms, shares the interpretations of famous spiritual leaders and scholars, and more. 5½ x 8½, 192 pp, Quality PB, ISBN 1-893361-28-4 **$16.95**

  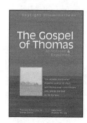 

The Way of a Pilgrim: *Annotated & Explained*
Translation and annotation by *Gleb Pokrovsky*

This classic of Russian spirituality is the delightful account of one man who sets out to learn the prayer of the heart—also known as the "Jesus prayer"—and how the practice transforms his life. 5½ x 8½, 160 pp, Illus., Quality PB, ISBN 1-893361-31-4 **$14.95**

The Gospel of Thomas: *Annotated & Explained*
Translation and annotation by *Stevan Davies*

Discovered in 1945, this collection of aphoristic sayings sheds new light on the origins of Christianity and the intriguing figure of Jesus, portraying the Kingdom of God as a present fact about the world, rather than a future promise or future threat. This edition guides you through the text with annotations that focus on the meaning of the sayings. 5½ x 8½, 192 pp, Quality PB, ISBN 1-893361-45-4 **$16.95**

Rumi and Islam: *Selections from His Stories, Poems, and Discourses—Annotated & Explained*
Translation and annotation by *Ibrahim Gamard*

Offers a new way of thinking about Rumi's poetry. Ibrahim Gamard focuses on Rumi's place within the Sufi tradition of Islam, providing you with insight into the mystical side of the religion—one that has love of God at its core and sublime wisdom teachings as its pathways. 5½ x 8½, 240 pp, Quality PB, ISBN 1-59473-002-4 **$15.99**

SkyLight Illuminations Series
Andrew Harvey, series editor

Zohar: *Annotated & Explained*
Translation and annotation by *Daniel C. Matt*

The cornerstone text of Kabbalah.

The best-selling author of *The Essential Kabbalah* brings together in one place the most important teachings of the *Zohar*, the canonical text of Jewish mystical tradition. Guides you step by step through the midrash, mystical fantasy, and Hebrew scripture that make up the *Zohar*, explaining the inner meanings in facing-page commentary. Ideal for readers without any prior knowledge of Jewish mysticism.

5½ x 8½, 176 pp, Quality PB, ISBN 1-893361-51-9 **$15.99**

Selections from the Gospel of Sri Ramakrishna
Annotated & Explained
Translation by *Swami Nikhilananda;* Annotation by *Kendra Crossen Burroughs*

The words of India's greatest example of God-consciousness and mystical ecstasy in recent history.

Introduces the fascinating world of the Indian mystic and the universal appeal of his message that has inspired millions of devotees for more than a century. Selections from the original text and insightful yet unobtrusive commentary highlight the most important and inspirational teachings. Ideal for readers without any prior knowledge of Hinduism.

5½ x 8½, 240 pp, b/w photographs, Quality PB, ISBN 1-893361-46-2 **$16.95**

 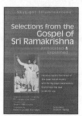  

Dhammapada: *Annotated & Explained*
Translation by *Max Müller* and revised by *Jack Maguire;* Annotation by *Jack Maguire*

The classic of Buddhist spiritual practice.

The Dhammapada—words spoken by the Buddha himself over 2,500 years ago—is notoriously difficult to understand for the first-time reader. Now you can experience it with understanding even if you have no previous knowledge of Buddhism. Enlightening facing-page commentary explains all the names, terms, and references, giving you deeper insight into the text.

5½ x 8½, 160 pp, b/w photographs, Quality PB, ISBN 1-893361-42-X **$14.95**

Hasidic Tales: *Annotated & Explained*
Translation and annotation by *Rabbi Rami Shapiro*

The legendary tales of the impassioned Hasidic rabbis.

The allegorical quality of Hasidic tales can be perplexing. Here, they are presented as stories rather than parables, making them accessible and meaningful. Each demonstrates the spiritual power of unabashed joy, offers lessons for leading a holy life, and reminds us that the Divine can be found in the everyday. Annotations explain theological concepts, introduce major characters, and clarify references unfamiliar to most readers.

5½ x 8½, 240 pp, Quality PB, ISBN 1-893361-86-1 **$16.95**

Children's Spirituality

Because Nothing Looks Like God
by *Lawrence and Karen Kushner*
Full-color illus. by *Dawn W. Majewski*

For ages 4 & up

MULTICULTURAL, NONDENOMINATIONAL, NONSECTARIAN

Real-life examples of happiness and sadness—from goodnight stories, to the hope and fear felt the first time at bat, to the closing moments of life—introduce children to the possibilities of spiritual life. A vibrant way for children—and their adults—to explore what, where, and how God is in our lives.

11 x 8½, 32 pp, HC, Full-color illus., ISBN 1-58023-092-X **$16.95**

Also available: **Teacher's Guide,** 8½ x 11, 22 pp, PB, ISBN 1-58023-140-3 **$6.95** For ages 5–8

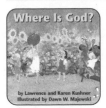

Where Is God? (A Board Book)
For ages 0–4

by *Lawrence and Karen Kushner*; Full-color illus. by *Dawn W. Majewski*

A gentle way for young children to explore how God is with us every day, in every way. Abridged from *Because Nothing Looks Like God* by Lawrence and Karen Kushner and specially adapted to board book format to delight and inspire young readers.

5 x 5, 24 pp, Board, Full-color illus., ISBN 1-893361-17-9 **$7.95**

What Does God Look Like? (A Board Book)
For ages 0–4

by *Lawrence and Karen Kushner*; Full-color illus. by *Dawn W. Majewski*

A simple way for young children to explore the ways that we "see" God. Abridged from *Because Nothing Looks Like God* by Lawrence and Karen Kushner and specially adapted to board book format to delight and inspire young readers.

5 x 5, 24 pp, Board, Full-color illus., ISBN 1-893361-23-3 **$7.95**

How Does God Make Things Happen? (A Board Book)
For ages 0–4

by *Lawrence and Karen Kushner*; Full-color illus. by *Dawn W. Majewski*

A charming invitation for young children to explore how God makes things happen in our world. Abridged from *Because Nothing Looks Like God* by Lawrence and Karen Kushner and specially adapted to board book format to delight and inspire young readers.

5 x 5, 24 pp, Board, Full-color illus., ISBN 1-893361-24-1 **$7.95**

What Is God's Name? (A Board Book)
For ages 0–4

by *Sandy Eisenberg Sasso*; Full-color illus. by *Phoebe Stone*

Everyone and everything in the world has a name. What is God's name? Abridged from the award-winning *In God's Name* by Sandy Eisenberg Sasso and specially adapted to board book format to delight and inspire young readers.

5 x 5, 24 pp, Board, Full-color illus., ISBN 1-893361-10-1 **$7.99**

Children's Spiritual Biography

Ten Amazing People
And How They Changed the World

For ages 7 & up

by *Maura D. Shaw*; Foreword by *Dr. Robert Coles*
Full-color illus. by *Stephen Marchesi*

Black Elk • Dorothy Day • Malcolm X • Mahatma Gandhi •
Martin Luther King, Jr. • Mother Teresa • Janusz Korczak •
Desmond Tutu • Thich Nhat Hanh • Albert Schweitzer

This vivid, inspirational, and authoritative book will open new possibilities for children by telling the stories of how ten of the past century's greatest leaders changed the world in important ways.

8½ x 11, 48 pp, HC, Full-color illus., ISBN 1-893361-47-0 **$17.95**

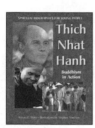 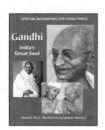 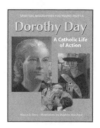

A new series: Spiritual Biographies for Young People

Thich Nhat Hanh: *Buddhism in Action*

For ages 7 & up

by *Maura D. Shaw*; Full-color illus. by *Stephen Marchesi*

Warm illustrations, photos, age-appropriate activities, and Thich Nhat Hanh's own poems introduce a great man to children in a way they can understand and enjoy. Includes a list of important Buddhist words to know.

6¾ x 8¾, 32 pp, HC, Full-color illus., ISBN 1-893361-87-X **$12.95**

Gandhi: *India's Great Soul*

For ages 7 & up

by *Maura D. Shaw*; Full-color illus. by *Stephen Marchesi*

There are a number of biographies of Gandhi written for young readers, but this is the only one that balances a simple text with illustrations, photographs, and activities that encourage children and adults to talk about how to make changes happen without violence. Introduces children to important concepts of freedom, equality, and justice among people of all backgrounds and religions.

6¾ x 8¾, 32 pp, HC, Full-color illus., ISBN 1-893361-91-8 **$12.95**

Dorothy Day: *A Catholic Life of Action*

For ages 7 & up

by *Maura D. Shaw*; Full-color illus. by *Stephen Marchesi*

Introduces children to one of the most inspiring women of the twentieth century, a down-to-earth spiritual leader who saw the presence of God in every person she met. Includes practical activities, a timeline, and a list of important words to know.

6¾ x 8¾, 32 pp, HC, Full-color illus., ISBN 1-59473-011-3 **$12.99**

Meditation/Prayer

Finding Grace at the Center: *The Beginning of Centering Prayer*

by *M. Basil Pennington*, OCSO, *Thomas Keating*, OCSO, and *Thomas E. Clarke*, SJ

The book that helped launch the Centering Prayer "movement." Explains the prayer of *The Cloud of Unknowing*, posture and relaxation, the three simple rules of centering prayer, and how to cultivate centering prayer throughout all aspects of your life.

5 x 7¼,112 pp, HC, ISBN 1-893361-69-1 **$14.95**

Prayers to an Evolutionary God

by *William Cleary*; Afterword by *Diarmuid O'Murchu*

How is it possible to pray when God is dislocated from heaven, dispersed all around us, and more of a creative force than an all-knowing father? In this unique collection of eighty prose prayers and related commentary, William Cleary considers new ways of thinking about God and the world around us. Inspired by the spiritual and scientific teachings of Diarmuid O'Murchu and Teilhard de Chardin, Cleary reveals that religion and science can be combined to create an expanding view of the universe—an evolutionary faith.

6 x 9, 208 pp, HC, ISBN 1-59473-006-7 **$21.99**

 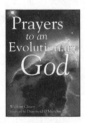  

Meditation without Gurus
A Guide to the Heart of Practice

by *Clark Strand*

Short, compelling reflections show you how to make meditation a part of your daily life, without the complication of gurus, mantras, retreats, or treks to distant mountains. This enlightening book strips the practice down to its essential heart—simplicity, lightness, and peace—showing you that the most important part of practice is not whether you can get in the full lotus position, but rather your ability to become fully present in the moment.

5½ x 8½, 192 pp, Quality PB, ISBN 1-893361-93-4 **$16.95**

Meditation & Its Practices
A Definitive Guide to Techniques and Traditions of Meditation in Yoga and Vedanta

by *Swami Adiswarananda*

The complete sourcebook for exploring Hinduism's two most time-honored traditions of meditation.

Drawing on both classic and contemporary sources, this comprehensive sourcebook outlines the scientific, psychological, and spiritual elements of Yoga and Vedanta meditation.

6 x 9, 504 pp, HC, ISBN 1-893361-83-7 **$34.95**

Spiritual Practice

The Sacred Art of Bowing
Preparing to Practice
by *Andi Young*

This informative and inspiring introduction to bowing—and related spiritual practices—shows you how to do it, why it's done, and what spiritual benefits it has to offer. Incorporates interviews, personal stories, illustrations of bowing in practice, advice on how you can incorporate bowing into your daily life, and how bowing can deepen spiritual understanding.
5½ x 8½, 128 pp, b/w illus., Quality PB, ISBN 1-893361-82-9 **$14.95**

Praying with Our Hands: *Twenty-One Practices of Embodied Prayer from the World's Spiritual Traditions*
by *Jon M. Sweeney*; Photographs by *Jennifer J. Wilson*;
Foreword by *Mother Tessa Bielecki*; Afterword by *Taitetsu Unno, PhD*

A spiritual guidebook for bringing prayer into our bodies.

This inspiring book of reflections and accompanying photographs shows us twenty-one simple ways of using our hands to speak to God, to enrich our devotion and ritual. All express the various approaches of the world's religious traditions to bringing the body into worship. Spiritual traditions represented include Anglican, Sufi, Zen, Roman Catholic, Yoga, Shaker, Hindu, Jewish, Pentecostal, Eastern Orthodox, and many others.
8 x 8, 96 pp, 22 duotone photographs, Quality PB, ISBN 1-893361-16-0 **$16.95**

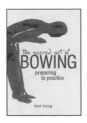   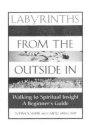

The Sacred Art of Listening
Forty Reflections for Cultivating a Spiritual Practice
by *Kay Lindahl*; Illustrations by *Amy Schnapper*

More than ever before, we need to embrace the skills and practice of listening. You will learn to: Speak clearly from your heart • Communicate with courage and compassion • Heighten your awareness for deep listening • Enhance your ability to listen to people with different belief systems. 8 x 8, 160 pp, Illus., Quality PB, ISBN 1-893361-44-6 **$16.99**

Labyrinths from the Outside In
Walking to Spiritual Insight—A Beginner's Guide
by *Donna Schaper* and *Carole Ann Camp*

The user-friendly, interfaith guide to making and using labyrinths— for meditation, prayer, and celebration.

Labyrinth walking is a spiritual exercise *anyone* can do. This accessible guide unlocks the mysteries of the labyrinth for all of us, providing ideas for using the labyrinth walk for prayer, meditation, and celebrations to mark the most important moments in life. Includes instructions for making a labyrinth of your own and finding one in your area.
6 x 9, 208 pp, b/w illus. and photographs, Quality PB, ISBN 1-893361-18-7 **$16.95**

Kabbalah

Honey from the Rock
An Introduction to Jewish Mysticism
by *Lawrence Kushner*

An insightful and absorbing introduction to the ten gates of Jewish mysticism and how it applies to daily life. "The easiest introduction to Jewish mysticism you can read."
6 x 9, 176 pp, Quality PB, ISBN 1-58023-073-3 **$16.95**

Eyes Remade for Wonder
The Way of Jewish Mysticism and Sacred Living
A Lawrence Kushner Reader
Intro. by *Thomas Moore*, author of *Care of the Soul*

Whether you are new to Kushner or a devoted fan, you'll find inspiration here. With samplings from each of Kushner's works, and a generous amount of new material, this book is to be read and reread, each time discovering deeper layers of meaning in our lives.
6 x 9, 240 pp, Quality PB, ISBN 1-58023-042-3 **$18.95**; HC, ISBN 1-58023-014-8 **$23.95**

Invisible Lines of Connection
Sacred Stories of the Ordinary
by *Lawrence Kushner* AWARD WINNER!

Through his everyday encounters with family, friends, colleagues and strangers, Kushner takes us deeply into our lives, finding flashes of spiritual insight in the process.
5½ x 8½, 160 pp, Quality PB, ISBN 1-879045-98-2 **$15.95**

Finding Joy
A Practical Spiritual Guide to Happiness
by *Dannel I. Schwartz* with *Mark Hass* AWARD WINNER!

Explains how to find joy through a time honored, creative—and surprisingly practical—approach based on the teachings of Jewish mysticism and Kabbalah.
6 x 9, 192 pp, Quality PB, ISBN 1-58023-009-1 **$14.95**; HC, ISBN 1-879045-53-2 **$19.95**

The Gift of Kabbalah:
Discovering the Secrets of Heaven, Renewing Your Life on Earth
by *Tamar Frankiel*, Ph.D.

Makes accessible the mysteries of Kabbalah. Traces Kabbalah's evolution in Judaism and shows us its most important gift: a way of revealing the connection between our "everyday" life and the spiritual oneness of the universe.
6 x 9, 256 pp, Quality PB, ISBN 1-58023-141-1 **$16.95**; HC, ISBN 1-58023-108-X **$21.95**

Spirituality

Journeys of Simplicity
Traveling Light with Thomas Merton, Bashō, Edward Abbey, Annie Dillard & Others
by *Philip Harnden*

There is a more graceful way of traveling through life.

Offers vignettes of forty "travelers" and the few ordinary things they carried with them—from place to place, from day to day, from birth to death. What Thoreau took to Walden Pond. What Thomas Merton packed for his final trip to Asia. What Annie Dillard keeps in her writing tent. What an impoverished cook served M. F. K. Fisher for dinner. Much more.

"'How much should I carry with me?' is the quintessential question for any journey, especially the journey of life. Herein you'll find sage, sly, wonderfully subversive advice."
—Bill McKibben, author of *The End of Nature* and *Enough*
5 x 7¼, 128 pp, HC, ISBN 1-893361-76-4 **$16.95**

The Alphabet of Paradise
An A–Z of Spirituality for Everyday Life
by *Howard Cooper*

"An extraordinary book." —Karen Armstrong

One of the most eloquent new voices in spirituality, Howard Cooper takes us on a journey of discovery—into ourselves and into the past—to find the signposts that can help us live more meaningful lives. In twenty-six engaging chapters—from A to Z—Cooper spiritually illuminates the subjects of daily life, using an ancient Jewish mystical method of interpretation that reveals both the literal and more allusive meanings of each. Topics include: Awe, Bodies, Creativity, Dreams, Emotions, Sports, and more.
5 x 7¼, 224 pp, Quality PB, ISBN 1-893361-80-2 **$16.95**

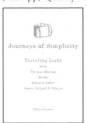 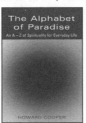 

Winter: A Spiritual Biography of the Season
Edited by *Gary Schmidt* and *Susan M. Felch*; Illustrations by *Barry Moser*

Explore how the dormancy of winter can be a time of spiritual preparation and transformation.

In thirty stirring pieces, *Winter* delves into the varied feelings that winter conjures in us, calling up both the barrenness and the beauty of the natural world in wintertime. Includes selections by Will Campbell, Rachel Carson, Annie Dillard, Donald Hall, Ron Hansen, Jane Kenyon, Jamaica Kincaid, Barry Lopez, Kathleen Norris, John Updike, E. B. White, and many others.

"This outstanding anthology features top-flight nature and spirituality writers on the fierce, inexorable season of winter.... Remarkably lively and warm, despite the icy subject."
—★*Publishers Weekly* Starred Review
6 x 9, 288 pp, 6 b/w illus., Deluxe PB w/flaps, ISBN 1-893361-92-6 **$18.95**
HC, ISBN 1-893361-53-5 **$21.95**